DATE DUE

ENTERED MAR 2 5 1997

Language,
Culture,
and Power

The poem on page 80 entitled "Under the Cover of Darkness,"
is printed with permission of Sis-Obed Torres Cordero.

Published by
State University of New York Press

© 1997   State University of New York

For information, address the State University of New York Press,
State University Plaza, Albany, NY 12246

Production by Bernadine Dawes • Marketing by Bernadette LaManna

Library of Congress Cataloguing-in-Publication Data

Soto, Lourdes Diaz, 1945-
    Language, culture, and power : bilingual families and the struggle
for quality education / Lourdes Diaz Soto : with a foreword by
Christine E. Sleeter.
        p.   cm. — (SUNY series, the social context of education)
    Includes bibliographical references (p. 157) and index.
    ISBN 0-7914-3141-X (hc : acid free). — ISBN 0-7914-3142-8 (pb :
acid free)
    1. Education, Bilingual—Social aspects—United States—Case
studies. 2. Bilingualism—United States—Case studies. I. Title.
II. Series: SUNY series, social context of education.
LC3731.S667 1997
370.117'0973—dc20   96-34721
                                                                    CIP

1 2 3 4 5 6 7 8 9 10

Language, Culture, and Power

BILINGUAL FAMILIES AND THE STRUGGLE
FOR QUALITY EDUCATION

LOURDES DIAZ SOTO

with a foreword by
CHRISTINE E. SLEETER

STATE UNIVERSITY OF NEW YORK PRESS

To my family, especially

Daniel Enrique

Deane Gian-Carlo, and

George Diaz,

whose love and support

have been a source of inspiration.

CONTENTS

What do the most successful teachers, schools of language, and ethnic-minority students do? What does their practice "look like"? Where can educators gain the most useful insights for teaching "other people's children" (Delpit 1995)? Educators with whom I talk around the country want answers to questions about what to do. At the same time, it continues to amaze me how often many express suspicion about and resist my answers to the questions about where to go for insights: the children, themselves, their parents, and other adults in their communities. In this excellent case study of the Puerto Rican community in an industrial city, Lourdes Diaz Soto exposes the painful conflicts surrounding the education of language- and ethnic- minority children, and the resistance of many Anglo educators and citizens toward successful teaching practices as well as toward parents and community as sources of knowledge. As Soto argues clearly, this is a political issue as much as it is an educational one. Further, the study reported here is far from being an isolated instance. Rather, it exemplifies far too much of life for communities of color in the 1980s and 1990s.

This is an era in which gains from the struggles of the 1960s and 1970s are being dismantled. In a four-part series of articles, Noam Chomsky (1995) examined in detail what he views as "the transition from containment of democracy and human rights to actual rollback" (p. 24). Affirmative action, aid to poor people, bilingualism, immigration, student loans, environmental protection, access to health care, funding for schools—these have become targets of a new conservatism that amounts to class warfare of the "haves" against "have-nots," and of white America reinstating white privileges and power. In popular discourse, rollbacks are often justified as being reasonable responses to programs that don't work. The problem is, such justification runs smack against both scholarly research and the insights and wisdom of groups who are losing what they have struggled for. And, ironically, the rights, programs, and forms of action being dismantled were fought for to serve the very purpose of gaining autonomy and self-sufficiency.

This book serves as a case study of such a rollback. Its focus is bilingual education and, more broadly, educational programming and practices that serve language- and cultural-minority children. Over the past few years several studies of successful teachers and schools of ethnic- and language-minority children have yielded a consistent profile (Ladson-Billings 1994; Haberman 1995; Garcia 1988; Lucas, Henze, & Donato 1990). Successful teachers share a mind-set and an attitudinal disposition toward the children and their community that includes:

- Unshakable belief in the children and their ability to learn
- Ability to communicate to the children that the teacher is clearly on their side
- High expectations for achievement with no excuses
- Orientation towards the community: its strengths, its culture, and its people
- Willingness to consult adults who are members of the children's racial or ethnic group
- Political interpretation of the community, its context in the large society, and the debilitating consequences of powerlessness and poverty

Successful teachers share the following areas of pedagogical knowledge and skill:

- Constructivist pedagogy that actively involves children in constructing knowledge; skill in "scaffolding" or building connections between what children already know and new knowledge
- Skill in using cooperative learning
- Ability to create curriculum that connects to and affirms the culture of the students
- Skill in using children's linguistic strengths to teach a second language or dialect, in a way that builds on rather than obliterates their first language or dialect
- Strong academic content knowledge and ability to create a challenging academic curriculum.

While parents and other community members usually cannot evoke professional terminology or cite the research literature, their sensibilities about how their own children learn best very often overlap with the research literature. That was clearly the case in the study reported in this book. Lourdes Diaz Soto identified and interviewed bilingual Puerto Rican adults who had achieved success in the community, and asked them to describe their own experiences with schooling and their advice for schools attempting to educate bilingual children. Their advice overlapped strongly with the research on effective teaching. For example, their descriptions of "quality programs" emphasized high academic expectations, active teaching strategies, affirmation of children's culture and language, and regular communication with the parents. These successful adults noted that such programs are already provided to children from privileged backgrounds; they were not advocating something different for children in their own community but rather for adaptations of such programs to their particular linguistic and cultural strengths. Puerto Rican parents in the community who had not attained high levels of education themselves shared the strong desire that schools should educate their children well, as well as the deep concern and frustration that the schools were not doing so. In addition, they were able to suggest ideas as to what the schools should do differently to teach their own children more effectively.

According to the research, successful schools are those in which educators, parents, and community members collaborate to support children developmentally (Comer 1988). Based on their review of research on families, schools, and communities, Nitza Hidalgo and her colleagues (1995) argue that "The concept of 'partnership' acknowledges that neither families nor schools alone can educate and socialize children for their work in society" (p. 515). While both research and practice have tended to focus on failures of children and their families, schools that have constructed the most successful working relationships focus on successes and view families as important resources to learning. These researchers note that "well-designed programs of partnership" pay off in educational benefits to the children. Through partnerships, schools use the knowledge communities have in order to construct programs that work best for the children.

> By contrast, weak or poorly designed programs exclude families who are from various cultures, label them "hard to reach," find them unresponsive, ignore their strengths, avoid their cultures and customs, deny their aspirations for their children or their knowledge of their children's talents, and treat them as part of (or as a cause of) their children's problems in school. Research suggests that when this happens, children suffer. (P. 517)

Paradoxically, school district administrators in this case study chose to exclude families and the educational programming the families advocated, and, by doing so, weaken the programming offered to language-minority children. Rather than viewing the Puerto Rican parents and other adults as a resource and source of insight, the white community and school administrators viewed them as potential trouble makers. Knowing this, the Puerto Rican adults had learned not to speak out for fear their children would suffer repercussions. They lived with their silence until the district attempted to close the school's bilingual program and implement English-only instruction. This excellent ethnographic study presents what happened when parents broke their silence and attempted to influence school policy.

This book grapples with the question of why professional educators, school-boards, and the broader community persistently refuse to listen to advice within communities of color regarding the education of their own children. If schools are failing to educate, if parents and other adults in the community can suggest what schools should be doing, and if their advice is supported by the research literature, why do members of the dominant society so often ignore or refuse to listen to such advice? In some cases, the advice of educators of color contradicts practices that "work" with Anglo children, and beliefs of Anglo teachers about how teaching should go (Delpit 1995; Reyes 1992). In many cases, the parents are not able to articulate their insights using the language and terminology that professional educators use, and thus, their ideas are dismissed. In my own work with teachers, I have heard them voice the belief that since they are professionally trained and parents are not, they—the teachers—know better than parents how classrooms should operate. Educators seem to view their own knowledge as superior, particularly if the parents have not themselves attained high levels of education. This belief too often persists, even when the children are not achieving well in school.

Multicultural and bilingual education connects to political issues involving voice and power, not just in schools but also in the wider society. Even though good bilingual education promotes educational achievement and English acquisition, it also supports bilingualism, which many monolingual Americans regard as anti-English and anti-American (a view which itself reflects historic amnesia). It is the political dimension of bilingualism, bilingual schooling, and empowering education that Soto examines in this book. Soto wants readers to feel outrage at the denigration this Puerto Rican community experienced, and to join struggles to maintain, develop, and expand gains in rights, access, and power that were made two decades ago. In so doing, she strongly affirms America's espoused ideals of freedom and democracy. She hopes that we will reexamine our own relationships with culturally diverse communities in our own work contexts, and construct relationships based on respect, dialog, and power sharing, both inside schools and in the wider society. Ultimately, this book passionately invites educators to support and collaborate with oppressed communities, for the purpose of successfully educating children. In the long run, the interconnected futures of all of our children is what is at stake.

REFERENCES

Chomsky, N. (1995). Rollback IV. *Z Magazine 8*(5). 18–24.

Comer, J.P. (1988). Educating poor minority children. *Scientific American 259*(5), 42–48.

Delpit, L. (1995). *Other people's children*. New York: The New Press.

Garcia, E. E. (1988). Attributes of effective teachers for language minority students. *Education and Urban Society 20*(4), 387-399.

Haberman, M. (1995). *Star teachers of children in poverty*. West Lafayette, Ind.: Kappa Delta Pi.

Hildago, N. M., Bright, J. A., Siu, S. F., Swap. S. W., & Epstein, J. L. (1995). Research on families, schools, and communities: A multicultural perspective. In J. A. Banks & C. A. M. Banks (Eds.), *Handbook of research on multicultural education.*, New York: Macmillan.

Ladson-Billings, G. (1994). *The dreamkeepers.* New York: Jossey-Bass.

Lucas, T., Henze, R., & Donato, R. (1990). Promoting the success of Latino language-minority students: An exploratory study of six high schools. *Harvard Educational Review 60*(3), 315–340.

Reyes, M. (1992). Challenging venerable assumptions: Literacy instruction for linguistically different students. *Harvard Educational Review 62*(4), 427–446.

ACKNOWLEDGMENTS

My deepest gratitude is expressed to the families who demonstrated a willingness to share themselves and their lives with so much generosity. I extend my warmest appreciation to Iris Cintron, Sergia Monz, Fred Rooney, Sis Obed Cordero, and Father Grabish, whose courage and willingness to struggle on behalf of children's equitable treatment are commendable. The active parents and community leaders whose voices were filled with optimism are the true light that shines in Steel Town.

I am indebted to the Spencer Foundation, whose assistance proved valuable in supporting my data collection and analysis. I am beholden to the influence and work of my professional colleagues, especially Lily Wong Fillmore, Christie Sleeter, and Antonia Lopez, whose support and encouragement have proved invaluable to me both professionally and personally. The work of James Crawford, Jim Cummins, and Eugene Garcia has contributed to my thinking about the field of bilingual education. I am grateful to Priscilla Ross and the readers of the State University of New York Press for their generosity.

Special recognition is due to Belen Mendoza, Elena Santos, Matilde Garcia, Pedro Medina, Laure Bernard, Connie Ballard, Judy Turner, and Marcia Barone, graduate students who provided assistance, a forum for discussions, and encouragement. I would also like to thank Hazel Hunley, Pat Wilson, Sarita De Carlo, and Judy Nastase for their assistance with the editorial and last-minute details.

And I have for many years been indebted to my colleagues, friends, and students in the mainland and the island.

The pearl of justice is found in the heart of mercy.
—Catherine of Siena

PROLOGUE

For many Americans today, the incessant attack on bilingual education appears to be warranted. Discussions by the public at large do not center on research evidence or linguistic human rights. The idea of teaching children in languages other than English arouses fear and misconceptions. In a Texas courtroom, for example, the use of the home language became an issue in a child custody case (*New York Times,* August 30, 1995). Even presidential candidates and politicians are working hard to ensure that children in America receive an English-only education (National Association for Bilingual Education 1995). The future needs of our nation indicate that such a precedence is dangerous while historical accounts show that this has not always been the case (Crawford 1989, 1992).

Are current xenophobic attitudes toward education helping children to lead our nation into the new millennium? Are second language learners and monolingual speakers benefiting from existing English-only curriculums? How can families who have traditionally been bilingual and families who want their children to speak more than one language come to terms with these issues? Is linguistic repression the wisest language policy for a democratic nation?

Children and families who are speakers of second languages find themselves immersed in hostile educational and community settings. For the past nine years, bilingual families residing in Steel Town have shared their wisdom and knowledge with me about what constitutes quality educational experiences for their children. It became evident to me from interviews and observations at meetings that a coercive power structure in the community was silencing the voices of bilingual families. The families shared specific research-supported knowledge and attempted to impart this information to the schools and the community. This study describes how bilingual families struggled for an inclusive, quality education in Steel Town.

Steel Town is a community that is known for its historically rich ethnic traditions of culture and language. My initial interactions with this community were by long distance until four years ago, when members of the community and a small, private, mostly white university made it possible for me to become a part of its citizenry.

Among the people who first greeted me on my first day on the job were the custodians.

> We saw your name on the door. We wondered if you were one of us. We have been
> so excited to think that a fellow Latino might be coming here as a professor. We saw
> the little flag [Puerto Rican] in your office. . . . Most of the cleaning crew is Puerto
> Rican. Many, many are those who forget about their people when they become
> "important."

The excitement of the custodial staff about my being there and their humility touched my heart. But I was soon reminded of the inequities a person of "difference" experiences in this community through my daily business. My own taste of a community environment hostile to bilingual families included threatening phone calls to my home late at night as well as abusive treatment at the supermarket, department store, and local hospital. I was stopped by local police officers on five separate occasions in spite of the fact that I had been driving lawfully. My children relayed specific instances of the discriminatory treatment they received at the local public schools. Daniel, my elder son, attended the local high school for his senior year while I was interviewing families for this study. He recalled incidents that angered him and shared some of his personal pain and humiliation with me:

> In a way, it was a wake-up call to the real world. I felt as if I had transferred from
> Disney World to a no-man's world. The teachers and the kids [in his former school]
> have no idea how great they have it. The teachers in Steel Town have scarce
> resources and few materials—like the art teacher. I'll be honest with you. . . . I felt
> hurt a lot of the time, especially when they [teachers] always asked me for my pass
> [in the hallway], but they never asked the white kids. They challenged me quite a bit
> and there were times I wanted to punch more than a few people. The Puerto Rican
> kids are treated differently . . . badly . . . and even the white kids should be receiving
> more encouragement. The highest aspiration these kids have is to attend the com-
> munity college. . . . I suffered a lot, Mom, more than I have ever told you.

My own, albeit limited, personal negotiations in the community that were peppered with hostility helped me learn about the daily realities of discrimination families face in Steel Town. One experience soon after I arrived caught me by surprise and reflects my initial naiveté about acceptance by the community. I was invited to present information about bilingual education research to the Steel Town board of education. I prepared a simplified version of the research literature for the board members, using overhead transparencies and handouts at the meeting to provide details about the research findings and optimal bilingual programs. I was frankly stunned when two school board members actually walked out of my talk, while two others conversed during my presentation. I stopped to ascertain what the problem was, only to feel the sting of deliberate and ignorant attacks on the field of bilingual education. These initial experiences were hints of future events involving legitimacy and power that I would encounter in Steel Town.

Attempts to find the best placement for my youngest son at the local public schools also led to more difficult and eye-opening experiences as to our perceived "difference." I began to wonder just how ingrained racism and white supremacist attitudes were in the local public schools. When I asked one high school principal about the educational climate for children of color, he responded, "This is America, isn't it?" This statement helped me reflect on the prejudicial learning environment that children have experienced and the sadness of what Sleeter and Grant (1992) refer to as "business as usual" in our schools and communities, meaning that institutional racism prevails with little awareness or concern about it.

The inequalities that accompany the differences between and among the family systems within Steel Town became evident to me through both data collection and personal observation. These differences that separate the people of color and the white majority in this community were apparent in socioeconomic disparity, educational inequity, lack of access to positions of power, and an implicit and explicit, pervasive racist climate. It soon became evident to me that there is a need to disseminate information that will help shed light on the racist environment in this particular community in order to foster a vision for sharing the greater need for the greater good.

My participant observations with families in Steel Town as they are immersed in the complexities of daily realities created personal feelings that defy description. As I reached out for information from these people, I could not help but share in the moment and be touched by my fellow human beings. The ability to be an "insider" attempting to translate to "outsiders" is a challenging task both for a researcher and a human being. Catherine Emihovich (1994) notes how contemporary "scholars are operating at the margins where knowledge in the service of activism is contested, and where the traditional pose of detached, passionless scholar can no longer be maintained" (p. 199).

The purpose of this study was to illustrate the nature of education for bilingual learners through the use of the case study (ethnographic interviews and participant observations). Evidence is given about the nature of bilingual education from three sources: the pilot study group of informants, the "success stories" of interviews, and the documentation of events of the case study. The data show how bilingual families struggled to obtain a quality education for their children. The ultimate goal of this book is to afford voice to the families regarding their perspectives on bilingual education in their community. The wisdom that these families shared, along with our existing knowledge base in regard to bilingual education and education for diversity, can be valuable to schools and to the nation.

The central approach for presenting this study is to allow the families' daily realities to constitute a shared learning experience for the reader. This study represents a unique piece of social history and the lessons that can be learned from these experiences. This work is unfinished because the events have continued to evolve as have the lives of the participants.

1

Overview

How do educational institutions and communities impact the lives of bilingual families? The goal of this book is to provide insights about such an impact on the lives of families negotiating daily educational realities. Decades of research have shown what constitutes optimal educational programs for bilingual learners, yet this study reveals how coercive power was used to limit children's access to a quality education. This slice of local history shows families struggling to obtain an equitable education for their children.

This first chapter provides an overview of the book, the main ideas, and how these relate to the literature. Qualitative research methods were used for data collection and to uncover educational issues of language, culture, and power within the context of the family and the community setting. This study takes place somewhere in the Commonwealth of Pennsylvania, with pseudonyms safeguarding the identities of the participants and the community leaders. Although generalizations are not possible, it is my hope that this book will help inform the reader about the educational issues faced by bilingual/bicultural families in America.

Local political controversy surrounding bilingual education impacted data collection for this study when the local school board and the school superintendent eliminated a nationally recognized, twenty-year-old bilingual education program. At this point I made a decision to include participant observations at community meetings dealing with bilingual education. I was informed that the language-minority families were organizing themselves for the first time in the history of this community. I felt that the families exhibited wisdom, resilience, and courage in the midst of the political controversy. The voices of the bilingual parents, community leaders, bilingual educators, and, what is more important, the bilingual children rang out loudly but were disregarded and silenced by "more powerful" elements.

It was evident that current educational structures in the Steel Town community have encouraged the disenfranchisement of the less valued and less powerful. Paulo Freire's concept of banking (1985), where students are filled with predetermined knowledge disconnected from daily social realities, comes to mind. These complex relations among the "haves" and the "have-nots" have helped perpetuate an intergenerational policy of silence. The ability to shed light and succeed in situations darkened by oppression show that like the electric star in the city, bilingual families represent a shining light in this community.

Bilingual Education Research

Decades of educational research have shown best practices for teaching language minority to children (Ambert 1991; Au & Jordan 1981; Crawford 1989; Collier 1989; Cummins 1993; Delgado-Gaitan 1990; Erickson 1987; Hakuta 1986; Heath 1983; Krashen 1988; Lucas, Henze, & Donato 1991; Macias 1987; McLaughlin 1984; Mehan, Hubbard & Villanueva 1994; Moll & Diaz 1987; Ogbu 1978; Peal & Lambert 1962; Phillips 1983; Swain 1987; Soto 1993; Spindler & Spindler 1987; Trueba 1987; Trueba, Jacobs, & Kirton 1990, Willig 1985; Wong Fillmore 1991). Demographic trends and major reports document concern about how bilingual children fare in schools and later as adults attempting to contribute to their own success and that of our nation (Aspira's High School Dropout Study Fernandez, et al. 1989; Carrasquillo 1991; Chapa & Valencia 1993; Hodgkinson 1985; Miranda 1991; The Decade of the Hispanic: An Economic Retrospective Miranda & Quiroz 1990; National Commission on Secondary Education for Hispanics 1984; State of Hispanic America 1991; Yzaquirre 1992; U.S. Hispanics: Challenging Issues for the 1990s, Valdivieso & Davis 1989; Olsen 1993). The overriding issue stems from the inability of bilingual children to experience success in school, despite high parental educational expectations. It is the assumption of this book (perhaps a naive one) that schools and communities knowledgeable about research findings in the field will be better equipped to implement programs reflecting best educational practices.

It is not my intent to review all of the literature discussing bilingualism, but rather to underscore findings from bilingual education research that can add to our understanding of what constitutes best teaching practices. The field can be organized around three basic eras in bilingual education: (1) the "bilingual-handicap" era; (2) the "positive findings" era; and (3) the "newly evolving paradigms" era. These three periods help explicate best practices, the historical evolution of research paradigms within the field, and the research climate of the particular historical era.

First, the "bilingual-handicap" era denotes findings based on the notion that bilingualism was considered synonymous with deficiency. With the notable exception of case studies, the initial research viewing childhood bilingualism is responsible for creating what Cummins (1989) refers to as the "myth of the bilingual handicap." A biased philosophy permeated the literature by pointing to bilingual learners' inherent deficiencies and pathologies.

Major reviews (Darcy 1953; Jensen 1962; Weinreich 1953) of this era document not only the flawed research methodology but also the accompanying negative and biased results. Frequently cited in these works is the research conducted by Saer (1923), who failed to match bilingual and monolingual learners on demographic variables; Pintner and Arsenian (1937), who relied on the child's surname as the indication of bilingualism; and Smith (1939), who counted "errors" of second-language learners and then attributed "preschool speech retardation" to the use of two languages. Cummins (1976) and Peal and Lambert (1962) have shown the serious methodological flaws of the era, including careless sampling procedures, classifying of bilinguals by surname, comparisons of students labeled as "monolingual or bilingual," and reliance on intelligence testing.

The attitude of this earlier work was captured by Jensen (1962), who reviewed more than two hundred studies relating the disadvantages of childhood bilingualism. Such disadvantages cited in the literature included handicaps in speech development, emotional and intellectual difficulties, impaired originality of thought, handicapped on intelligence tests, loss of self-confidence, schizophrenia, and contempt and hatred toward one's parents, to name but a few. The advent of the psychometric tradition and the search for the measurement of intelligence also contributed to negative stereotypes of bilingual learners. Goodenough for example, stated, "Those nationality groups whose average intellectual ability is inferior do not readily learn the new language" (1926, 393).

Hakuta (1986) notes that it is important to view this early literature in light of historical debates in our nation over the quality of immigrant groups. There were notable exceptions in the bilingual-handicap era consisting of case studies such as Leopold's (1939). In general, however, this era viewed bilingualism as an independent variable contributing to both intellectual and emotional ill effects. The problem with the research era of the 1920s through the early 1960s is that in spite of additional contemporary research, it continues to drive existing programs employing subtractive practices. "Subtractive" is a term used by Lambert (1975) to denote deficit strategies that replace one language with another.

The "positive-findings" era was ushered in by Peal and Lambert's (1962) study of bilingual learners in Montreal. "The picture that emerges . . . is that of a youngster whose wider experiences in two cultures have given him advantages which a monolingual does not enjoy. Intellectually his experiences with two language systems seems to have left him with a mental flexibility, a superiority in concept formation, a more diverse field set of mental abilities"(20). A brighter, more positive view of bilingualism began to emerge as Peal and Lambert responded to previous research by accounting for language proficiency, controlling demographic variables, and documenting findings from previous studies.

The St. Lambert Project, a field study (Lambert & Tucker 1972), was largely responsible for confirming Peal and Lambert's (1962) findings and led the way for the initiation and replication of controlled experimental conditions by researchers in the United States and other countries. Examples of these studies indicated that:

(a) children raised bilingually were more attentive to semantic relationships than mono-linguals (Ianco-Worral 1972)
(b) bilingual children indicated superiority in awareness of linguistic rules and structures (Ben-Zeev 1977)

(c) bilingual children outperform monolinguals on a variety of measures of metalinguistic awareness (Cummins 1978)

(d) bilingualism has a positive effect on divergent thinking and creativity (Torrance, Wu, Gowan, & Alliotti 1970)

(e) bilingualism has positive effects on a variety of cognitive performance measures, such as concept formation (Cummins & Gulutsan 1974; Bain 1974; Liedtke & Nelson 1968)

(f) there are positive effects of bilingualism on Piagetian conservation and field independence (Duncan & De Avila 1979)

(g) bilinguals demonstrated an ability to monitor cognitive performance (Bain & Yu 1980)

(h) there is a significant contribution of second-language proficiency to cognitive measures, including the Raven Progressive Matrices (Hakuta & Diaz 1985)

(i) learning concepts in the native language will transfer and enhance second-language learning (Cummins 1979)

The experimental studies of the 1970s and early 1980s indicated the advantages of raising children bilingually. These studies documented the enhancing and positive effects of bilingualism on a variety of cognitive performance measures, metalinguistic attributes, divergent thinking, and creativity. These studies also modeled increasing knowledge about optimal quantitative research methodologies, focused on cognitive advantages, and proposed theoretical frameworks that helped guide future bilingual education research.

The era of "newly evolving paradigms" has benefited the field by providing broader conceptual frameworks and interdisciplinary research, particularly among educators and anthropologists. These studies have relied to a greater extent on qualitative methods and have initiated methods for viewing issues of language and culture as related domains. Findings from this era have helped us understand:

(a) the value of changing classroom interactions so that they are compatible with the home (Au & Jordan 1981)

(b) how critical analysis of classroom language (teacher–child interactions) can enhance children's learning (Cazden 1988)

(c) how communities in the same setting can be both similar and different in their contributions to the home and community language learning environment (Heath 1983)

(d) the discontinuities experienced by young Papago children entering their first preschool encounter and the accompanying teacher intervention strategies (Macias 1987)

(e) the effects of teacher assumptions about children's English language proficiency on the quality of instruction (Moll & Diaz 1985)

(f) why Native American children have been regarded as "quiet" (Phillips 1983)

(g) the importance of the distinction between social conversational language skills and the more complex cognitive academic skills (Cummins 1989)

(h) why the loss of the primary language, especially when it is the only language spoken by parents, can be costly to children, families, and society as a whole (Wong Fillmore 1992)

(i) the long-term benefits of bilingual education programs on children's attitudes (Collier 1991)

(j) how support for native-language instruction afforded young children an opportunity to outperform comparison groups (Krashen 1988)

(k) how the inclusion of the home language in a developmentally appropriate early childhood setting is beneficial to young children's growth and development (Paul & Jarvis 1992)

(l) how families who support the native language at home have "academically successful" young children in school (Soto 1993)

(m) the benefits of untracking high school programs for Latino/a and African American students' academic success (Mehan, Hubbard, & Villanueva 1994),

(n) the elements of six high schools that have promoted the academic achievement of Latino/a- minority students (Lucas, Henze, & Donato 1990).

The field of bilingual education is continuing to evolve, explore, and experiment with research methods, theoretical frameworks, and alternate paradigms (Soto 1992a, b). It is also becoming more evident to scholars that there is a need for social-science research in general to redirect itself from deficit/stereotypical paradigms to exploratory/creative paradigms capable of meeting the needs of minority teachers, learners, and families (Ernst & Statzner 1994).

The studies described in the last era have added a tremendous amount of knowledge and evidence regarding best educational practices. How is it, then, that schools and communities reflect such huge discrepancies between the existing knowledge base and the proliferation of oppressive programs? How can schools reconcile the fact that they are implementing programs that are harming children and families? How has public opinion and the English-only philosophy permeated the school curriculum?

The Politics of Bilingual Education

It is difficult to talk about bilingual education without viewing relevant political issues. James Crawford (1989, 1992) relates the historical and political context of bilingual education in America. He notes that German-language schools prevailed until the twentieth century and that historically significant documents such as the

Articles of Confederation were published in German and French. When the United States entered World War I, however, anti-German sentiment created language restrictions. Several states passed laws banning German speech, with at least 18,000 persons being criminally charged under these laws by 1921 (Crawford 1989). "Soon the fervor for Anglo-conformity spilled over into hostility toward all minority tongues" (24). Public attitudes toward languages changed as English-only speech became associated more and more with patriotism. In spite of the Supreme Court's ruling in *Meyer v. Nebraska* (1923) against restrictive language laws, minority languages have been devalued in the nation. Public schools responded to the climate and the politics of the times by implementing monolingual programs.

The federal government also mandated that Native Americans be taught in English only. The U.S. Senate documented that in the 1850s the Oklahoma Cherokees attained higher literacy levels in English than the white populations in Texas or Arkansas. In 1879, however, Native American children were being separated from their families and sent to militarizing boarding schools. U.S. Representative Ben Nighthorse Campbell from Colorado recounted, "Both my grandparents were forcibly removed from their homes and placed in boarding schools. One of the first English words Indian students learned was 'soap,' because their mouths were constantly being washed out for using their native language" (Crawford 1989, 25).

Mexican American and Asian children have been punished under the guise of English-only speech being patriotic. An early childhood educator and former migrant worker in California recently reported on a commonly accepted practice in the local public school:

> When our teacher caught us speaking our language, she would lock us in the closet. Sometimes there would be threee of us in that tiny space. It was dark and pretty frightening for us. Sometimes it was even hard to breathe in there. Other teachers punished the Spanish speakers at recess, lunch, or with after school "Spanish detention." (Lopez 1995)

Activities aimed at punishing children for speaking their native language still persist in contemporary America. In Louisiana, for example, children have been asked to kneel for speaking in a language other than English. In Pennsylvania, children have been held back a grade for speaking a language other than English. In California, children are expected to "prove" their national origin.

For Latino/a leaders, the concerted effort to mandate English-only is synonymous with an America that is for whites-only. Raul Yzaguirre of the National Council of La Raza stated, "U.S. English is to Hispanics as the Ku Klux Klan is to Blacks" (Crawford 1992, 149). The founders of the U.S. English-only movement include Dr. John Taton, a Michigan opthalmologist and population control activist.

The fear of loss of power by Anglos to minorities is expressed in a paper by Dr. Taton:

"Gobernar es poblar" translates "to govern is to populate." In this society, where the majority rules, does this hold? Will the present majority peaceably hand over its political power to a group that is simply more fertile? Can *homo contraceptivus* compete with *homo progenitiva?* Perhaps this is the first instance in which those with their pants up are going to get caught with their pants down. ... As Whites see their power and control over their lives declining, will they simply go quietly into the night? (Crawford 1989, 57)

In addition to the racist propaganda, there is evidence indicating monetary contributions to the English-only organization by advocates of eugenic sterilization (Crawford 1989). It is hard to believe that proponents of ethnic cleansing could ever exist in America.

The historical context and companion policies have institutionalized repressive language policies impacting the linguistic human rights of children and families. Questions that come to mind include: Why has English-only and monolingualism been associated with patriotism in America? Why are educated Americans less likely to speak a second language than educated Europeans, Canadians, Asians, or Africans? Why has it become increasingly difficult for the State Department to find competent translators and employees knowledgeable in languages and cultures? If researchers and scholars have addressed issues of what constitutes best teaching practices, why are schools so reluctant to implement them?

Cummins (1994) refers to the "new enemy within" as groups and individuals who continue to spread xenophobic perspectives. He compares our nation to the *Titanic* headed for destruction in regard to issues of bilingualism. Isolated programs of excellence are shedding light on best practices, yet these programs appear to be the exception and face tremendous barriers to implementation from agencies and the public at large.

The dissemination of information capable of inciting fear, divisiveness, and a racist agenda has created a climate that devalues bilingualism/biculturalism in this country. Language-minority populations understand the need to communicate in English–so much so that the loss of home languages in America is a concern documented by linguists (Veltman 1983; Wong Fillmore 1992). The advocates of cultural conservatism, the "enemies within," have also helped devalue bilingualism/biculturalism by advocating a knowledge base that is Anglo-centric and exclusionary.

English-plus alternatives have been long advocated by professional organizations such as the National Association for Bilingual Education, the National Council of Teachers of English, the Modern Language Association, the Teachers of English to Speakers of Other Languages, the Linguistic Society of America, and others. The idea that learners will benefit from knowledge that values languages and cultures is supported by the research literature, by global national interests, and by the vision of a well-educated, competitive society.

Benefits of Home Language

Historically, the sociopolitical context of the nation has contributed to crusades to eliminate bilingualism and institutionalize linguistic repression, yet native languages and native cultures are at the heart of the communicative process for families. Intergenerational communication is a vital part of child-rearing patterns that foster young children's social, emotional, and cognitive well-being. When parents, grand-parents, and extended family members lovingly impart values, beliefs, and cultural wisdom to children, those children can attain a healthy sense of self.

The loss of language and of intergenerational communication is a concern when reports indicate that as of 1990, 6.3 million children ages five to seventeen do not speak English at home. This figure represents a 38 percent increase over the past decade and indicates that the number of school-age children who do not speak English at home continues to rise (Zelasko 1993). The U.S. Census Bureau data (1991) show that 31.8 million people, or 14 percent of the population, indicated that they spoke a language other than English at home. Spanish speakers represent 54 percent of the language minority-population of this country.

In an article entitled "The Growth of Multilingualism and the Need for Bilingual Education: What Do We Know So Far?" Dorothy Waggoner (1993) documents increasing numbers of home-language speakers between 1980 and 1990 in the United States:

> More and more people in the United States speak languages other than English at home. Many languages were previously almost unknown in this country. The changes reflect the extent and character of recent immigration. They also reflect the natural growth of linguistic minority populations. While the number of monolingual English speakers increased by 6 percent in the 1980's, the number of home speakers of languages other than English (HSNELS) increased by 38 percent. The numbers of speakers of some of the Asian languages spoken by recent immigrants more than doubled. However, despite immigration, the majority of HSNELS are native born and natural growth is increasing the numbers of school-age HSNELS disproportionately in comparison with the numbers of school-age majority children. (1993, 1)

Tables presented by Waggoner show a decade of increasing proportions for speakers of Spanish, Asian-Indian languages, Chinese languages, Korean, Thai and Laotian, Vietnamese, Farsi, Filipino languages, Arabic, Armenian, Japanese, Portuguese, and Russian. Decreasing proportions were shown for speakers of American Indian and Alaskan native languages, Czech, French, German, Greek, Hungarian, Italian, Norwegian, Polish, Serbo-Croatian, Swedish, Ukrainian, and Yiddish. These data help illustrate the dramatic growth of multilingualism in America, as well as needed linguistic preservation. Our society can choose to view demographic trends through the lens of an oppressor or through the lens that views linguistic human rights and human resource potential.

Affording children and families the gift of home-language preservation has been documented as being beneficial in a variety of ways. Cummins notes that native-language instruction develops pride in one's identity, which in turn has been shown by research to be linked to school achievement (see Cummins 1979 for a review of these studies). Hakuta (1986) indicates that bilingual children have certain advantages that monolingual children do not have, one of the most important being "cognitive flexibility" or divergent thinking. Using children's home language as a medium of instruction is important because: (1) it supplies background knowledge that makes English more comprehensible; (2) it enhances the development of literacy since knowledge is transferred from the home language to the second language; and (3) first-language development has cognitive and practical advantages, and promotes a healthy sense of biculturalism (Krashen 1988).

What is the cost of language loss to families and society? Lily Wong Fillmore (1991), a linguist from the University of California–Berkeley, has studied the effects of early educational programs conducted in English only. She found that these programs result in the loss of the child's native language. In the NABE NO-Cost Study, Fillmore gathered data from families across the nation:

> What about the cost to the family and children? When what is lost is the means of communication in a family, the children lose access to all the things that parents can teach them. Where the parents are able to speak English, the loss is not complete. If the parents are willing to switch to English too, they can go on socializing their children in the values, beliefs, and practices that are important to the family and community. When the parents are not able to do so, what is lost is closeness and family unity. That may be too big a price for children to pay for an easier transition from home to school. (Wong Fillmore 1991, 42)

The notion of a home-language gift (maintaining and protecting home languages and cultures) can be viewed as part of a critical analysis of existing educational practices. Since the field of bilingual education research has shown the benefits of native language to both academic school success and the enhancement of family communication (Cummins 1979; Hakuta 1986; Krashen 1988; Wong Fillmore 1991), will it be important for schools and communities to implement programs reflecting these findings? At a time in our history when the nation discusses family values, should family communication and school success be important components of these discussions? Is a family's ability to communicate with their children in the "mother tongue" an important component of linguistic human rights? (Skutnabb-Kangas 1989). Could our nation benefit by viewing issues of language and culture within a linguistic human rights perspective?

Just as a person's gender will determine much of his or her future, so will birth as a child of color in America. Contemporary families face multiple, complex challenges within existing societal contexts with linguistically and culturally diverse families facing additional human rights issues. Can we afford to tolerate the current American social climate that devalues languages and cultures? How long will children and families have to remain in such a state of vulnerability?

Latino Families

Latino/as comprise the fastest-growing ethnic minority population in the United States. The 1990 Census showed a 50 percent increase in population growth for Latino/as compared to 9 percent for the total population. The Census figures indicate that there are 22.4 million Latino/as who comprise 9 percent of the nation's population. Mexican Americans constitute 60 percent of the Latino population while Puerto Ricans make up 12 percent (of the mainland Latino population), other Hispanics, 22 percent, and Cuban Americans, 5 percent. The age distribution for Latino/as indicates a median age of 26 compared to a non-Latino median age of 33.5. While demographers predict that the nation's youth (newborns to seventeen years of age) will increase by 17 percent Latino youth are expected to triple (Chapa & Valencia 1993). What does our nation need to know about Latino families?

For one, issues of language and culture have been an integral part of the history of Latino families in the United States. The history of linguistic and cultural preservation by Spanish-speaking families predates the arrival of English speakers to America. At the end of the Mexican-American War, for example, the Treaty of Guadalupe Hildalgo gave Spanish coequal status with English as the language of government in California and other territories ceded to the United States:

> Echoing the words of the Louisiana Purchase, the Treaty of Guadalupe Hidalgo provided that the new Spanish-speaking citizens of the United States "shall be maintained and protected in the free enjoyment of their liberty and property, and secured in the free exercise of their religion without restriction." For the Mexicans and, as events would show, for sympathetic norteamericanos, these promises implied some recognition of the Spanish language; its special role in the Southwest and its speakers' need for reasonable accommodations from their government. This did not mean official bilingualism—a strict equality of the two languages—but rather the equal protection of Spanish speakers under U.S. law, that is, unrestricted access to legislatures, courthouses, and schools regardless of their English-speaking ability. These were concessions comparable to what Louisianans had won. (Crawford 1992, 63)

The pre–Mexican-American War Spanish-speaking families of the Southwest were not recently arrived immigrants, but families who had been conquered and promised equal protection under the law. The monolingual Spanish-speaking families of Puerto Rico also predated English-speaking colonizers and have historically sought to protect their home language in their own land. Crawford notes that, by 1909,

> 607 out of Puerto Rico's 678 grade schools had been anglicized—an amazing feat at a time when English was spoken by only 3.6 percent of Puerto Ricans. While Spanish was retained as a subject, English became the basic medium of instruction. In practice this meant that children spent much of their time parroting a language they had no occasion to use outside of class, while other subjects were generally neglected. Predictably, most students left school before completing the third grade. . . . By 1913 the legislature was demanding the reinstatement of Spanish, but U.S. officials blocked the change. . . . The mandatory English policy would affect three generations of schoolchildren before it was finally scrapped, an acknowledged failure, in 1949. (P. 50)

It is evident that Latino families have tried to play by the rules in an effort to attain the American Dream. Latino families have worked hard and have contributed to the prosperity of the nation, yet the National Council of La Raza notes that:

(a) in spite of possessing typical American values such as loyalty to family, religious faith, a strong work ethic, and patriotism, Latino/as continue to be viewed negatively in public opinion polls and the media

(b) Latino/a children are three times more likely to be poor, even with a working, full-time, year-round parent

(c) Latino males have the highest labor force participation rate, yet are more likely to be among the working poor

(d) Latino/as have the lowest levels of educational attainment with only 50 percent completing high school (compared to 80 percent for non-Latinos), while one out of ten attains a college degree

(e) Latino/a children are underrepresented in preschool programs and other programs designed to help at-risk students (Yzaguirre 1992)

The economic restructuring of our nation has hit mainland Puerto Rican families especially hard since cities suffering the greatest industrial losses were also cities with the largest Puerto Rican population (Newark, New York, Chicago, Philadelphia). Data show that Puerto Rican families have the highest poverty rates in the nation at nearly 40 percent. It is alarming to note that one out of every two (56.7%) Puerto Rican children lives in poverty (Miranda 1991; National Puerto Rican Coalition 1992). Elizabeth Weiser Ramirez of Aspira notes:

> Statistics show Latino men and women are well represented in the work force, but they generally receive low wages. People are working full time, year round, but they

cannot sustain their families. A low number of Latinos have high levels of education, and the gap is increasing between wages for a person with a college degree and
a high school degree. (Gomez 1993)

In Steel Town, more than 40 percent of the population growth in the past
decade came from racial-/ethnic-minority families (Partnership for Community
Health 1993). The Governor's Advisory Commission on Latino Affairs indicated concern about the recurrent issues impacting Latino/a students residing in the
Commonwealth of Pennsylvania; for example:

(a) Latino/as have one of the highest dropout rates in the Commonwealth
(b) Latino/a students have a high rate of suspension, expulsion, and retention
(c) there is an overrepresentation of Latino/a students in some areas of special
     education and an underrepresentation in gifted programs
(d) there is a disproportionate number of Latino/a students tracked into lower
     academic/remedial courses
(e) there is a lack of evaluation data to substantiate the effectiveness of bilingual
     programs
(f) there are insufficient numbers of bilingual programs to serve the needs of
     limited English proficient students (Sanchez-Cintron 1993)

The data and reports describing how Latino families are faring in the Steel Town
community and the Commonwealth mirror the kind of patterns documented and
observed throughout the nation. It is evident that continued concern about how
Latino/a children are faring in schools and communities is warranted. These trends
make a case for the continued need to explore how current educational practices
impact family systems. In addition, there is an urgent need for creating an educational revolution with empowering agendas that will benefit families and children who
have consistently contributed to the fabric of our nation.

Methodological Approaches

The purpose of this book is to illustrate the nature of education for Latino/a learners
in Steel Town through the use of ethnographic interviews and participant observations. Evidence about the nature of education was documented from three sources: a
pilot study group of informants living in Steel Town, the "success stories" interviews
with professional families living in Steel Town and providing leadership to the community, and documentation of events leading to the dismantling of a bilingual education program.

I became interested in collaborating with bilingual families as a result of both
professional and personal experiences. I personally experienced what I can best
describe as "two worlds of childhood," one in a rural Puerto Rican community and

one in an urban mainland setting. This set the stage for early comparisons between life as an islander and life as a Newyorican. As a bilingual child I felt the tension and the contrast between two cultures. My roles as a mother, teacher, and grandmother have also helped shape personal, first hand knowledge about the "two worlds of childhood." All of these experiences have no doubt influenced much of my thinking and have led to an enthusiasm and passion for research that will allow "outsiders" to gain an understanding of the realities faced by Latino families and children in America.

My previous research with Puerto Rican families focused on the family's contribution to children's school achievement (Soto 1986–93). This book, however, departs from previous, mainly quantitative work in my attempt to search for alternate research paradigms, nondeficit perspectives (Soto 1992a, 1992b), and collaborative ties with families. The search for broader perspectives with in-depth descriptions has led me to pursue knowledge from the field of anthropology and from colleagues who have implemented qualitative research designs. This document in no way reflects my colleagues' perspectives but my own modest attempts to pursue "newly evolving bilingual research paradigms" capable of integrating a collaborative voice on behalf of bilingual families and children.

The present study viewing bilingual families and schooling is in many ways a labor of love, attempting to afford players a voice in the educational agendas of policy makers and educators. Anderson (1989) notes that reflexivity in critical ethnography involves a dialectical relationship among the researcher's constructs, the informants' constructs, the research data, the researcher's ideological biases, and structural and historical forces. These complex relations can be understood within a framework of daily family and community interactions as the researcher searches for significance, interprets data, and disseminates information. The ability and willingness of researchers (educators) to self reflect is critical in the evolving field of multicultural research (Soto 1992a). This type of activity places researchers in a state of vulnerability yet has potential for initiating alternative and experimental research paradigms.

The need to disseminate information about how schools impact bilingual children and bilingual families inspired the conceptual framework of this study. The initial research design was intended to comprise ethnographic interviews only but was broadened to include participant observations based on evolving events in the community. The Spencer Foundation provided a small grant for data collection and analysis. Ethnographic interviews (Spradley 1979, 1980) were conducted within the community context with a pilot sample of bilingual families first, and later with bilingual, educated professional families. The pilot sample was comprised of mothers of young children with low levels of education. I refer to the educated professional families as the "success stories" in this book, although all bilingual families can be thought of as "success stories" in light of their determination and ability to survive, often in hostile environments. Persons with these success stories have attained their professional educational goals, are upwardly mobile by their socioeconomic achievement, and contribute time, expertise, and money to the Steel Town community.

I used the developmental sequence suggested by Spradley for the interviews, while my data analyses followed the grounded theory procedures recommended by Strauss and Corbin (1990). My use of the grounded theory procedures revealed categories—(language, culture, power)—and the common themes shared by the informants. My data collection was influenced by the local school district's decision to eliminate a twenty-year-old, award-winning bilingual education program.

When bilingual education became a controversy in the community, I included participant observations (Spradley 1980) to help explain how bilingual families have sought a quality education for their children in Steel Town. I received additional inspiration for this study from Patty Lather's reference (1986) to catalytic validity or "the degree which the research process re-orients, focuses, and energizes participants in what Freire terms 'conscientization'" (1970, 67).

Researchers working and living in community settings may find Lather's reference to catalytic validity an important area for further consideration. Is it important to draw lines in the sand among our multiple roles? Are there ethical guidelines that can help to supersede historical roles of researchers as oppressors? Should we ensure that communities benefit from our presence, or is our primary goal to "tell the story"? I struggled with these questions and found myself leaning toward an objective stance as a "storyteller," if you will. When community members asked me for information and knowledge about the field, I readily availed myself but felt that they owned any decision making regarding avenues that needed to be pursued.

Ultimately, qualitative research methods afforded me an opportunity to gain the bilingual family's perspective and to engage in participant–researcher collaboration. Pilot families were asked to share their views about how schools impact their children's education. The mutual areas of participant–researcher concern assisted with data collection and included tape-recorded interviews with the pilot set of families and later in the homes of educated professionals. In addition, I conducted participant observations at community meetings, gathered documents disseminated by the school district, and analyzed one calendar year of newspaper accounts reporting the bilingual controversy in Steel Town. A "snowballing" effect occurred when the initial pilot interviewees nominated educated, professional bilingual families who were respected by the Latino community. "You know who you should talk to about this. . . . Why don't you interview . . . ?" The element of respect/*respeto* appeared important to the families who nominated subsequent families for interviews.

The interrrelationship of experiences, perceptions, and perspectives of bilingual families interacting with schools within the context of Steel Town comprise this historical account. This study found that power continues to limit children's access to a quality education, in spite of documentation by bilingual education research about what constitute optimal programs for language-minority children. Lisa Delpit (1993) describes aspects of power and suggests that an "appropriate education of poor children and children of color can only be devised in consultation with adults who share their culture" (138). The fundamental issue, Delpit maintains, is whose voice gets to be heard. The bilingual families in this study were not a part of a consultation process prior to the implementation of decisions affecting Latino/a children in Steel Town such as busing and programmatic decisions. The educated participant-informants consciously perceived the distinctions between oppressed and oppressors. They described their frustrations and past experiences with schools and disclosed events that were obviously painful to recall.

What is it like for bilingual families living in Steel Town? Chapter 2 describes the community context, including the history of Steel Town and how Latino families were recruited to the area as migrant workers and temporary laborers for the steel industry's coke ovens. Close to ten thousand Latino families still reside in Steel Town, with their children comprising 25 percent of the school population.

Chapter 3 presents the ethnographic interviews with educated professional Latino families. Excerpts of the interviews depict the voices of the participants and recurrent themes in language, culture, and power.

Chapter 4 explores the early schooling of bilingual children in Steel Town. This chapter shows how disparate are current educational practices with the research knowledge base. Examples of families' interactions with schools devaluing children's native language and culture are provided.

Chapter 5 shows salient events leading to the dismantling of a twenty-year-old, award-winning bilingual education program. The bilingual program in Steel Town was recognized by the Office of Education as a national program of excellence. The bilingual controversy that ensued shows interactions between families struggling for quality programs and the school officials who charted a course of systematic oppression.

Chapter 6 includes the analysis of one calendar year of local newspaper accounts that helped explain how the bilingual program became a political controversy in Steel Town. The push for English-only was apparent in the media, local stores, and the city council ordinances of nearby Post Town.

Chapter 7 explores the issues of language, culture, and power along with a theoretical framework that initiates discussion about the complex relations limiting language-minority children's access to a quality education.

The epilogue includes an update of the lives of the players in this study. Their lives have been impacted by the bilingual controversy and have continued to evolve.

The appendixes include information relating to the dismantling of the bilingual program in Steel Town: first, the initial study submitted by the school district's Bilingual Committee, entitled "Bilingual Program Recommendations"; second, the school superintendent's response to the latter report; and third, the school district's current program, entitled "A Ticket for Tomorrow."

The data gathered for this study reveal the complexities of power issues in the Steel Town community and its schools. This is but a small contribution revealing the uniqueness of the bilingual experience in America. How were families and children limited in their search for a quality education in Steel Town? The interviews with families, participant observations at community meetings, and portrayals in the media help document the inequities bilingual children face in America. Since one community is the focus of this study, generalizations to other settings and historical contexts may be limited. This book builds on the work of colleagues who have valiantly expressed needed truths so that future exploratory work could be pursued. The collaborative desire of educators in the field of bilingual education has been to ultimately afford knowledge about what constitutes quality educational programs for bilingual children. I only hope this research will in some small way become useful to communities hoping to focus on the educational needs of bilingual children.

2

The Community

"Swallowing Hard"

The community plays a vital part in a family's quality of life and a child's educational future. Bronfenbrenner's (1979) Russian nested-doll example, often cited in the literature, helps explain the various environments available to families and communities. The smallest inner-nested doll represents the smallest unit, the family, while the continued concentric circles represent the ever-widening community elements. Bronfenbrenner (1986) describes the alienation between young people and adults in a modern society in the "four worlds of childhood": family, friends, school, and work. There is no doubt that increasingly complex sociopolitical issues are continually impacting children, families, and communities within the ecological social context.

The variety of families residing in Steel Town are an integral part of the historical context, which is rich with language and culture. The view from its southern bridges shows the inherent physical diversity of the community. The smoke billowing from the huge, rust-colored metal buildings hint of the historical past of the steel industry. The Lehigh River divides the rolling hills of the South Side, dotted with small, attached wooden homes, brick buildings, and churches, from the pride-filled, historically rich cobbled streets and the northern suburban township.

The month of August brings visitors from nearby as well as faraway to partake in the summer activities. The major event is a musical celebration, Summerfest, which has continued to highlight the German roots of the region. A letter to the editor of the local newspaper (August 29, 1993) shows the exclusion of diverse kinds of music, especially Latino and African American:

> To the Editor:
>
> As a musician who grew up in Steel Town, I have always looked forward to Summerfest. Over the past years, however, I have noticed a diminishing variety of types of music and sorts of people in the festival. I remember when Latin, reggae, blues and African music were more prominently featured. These styles are not just where my musical preferences lie; they brought a more diverse, multi-cultural crowd to downtown Steel Town.
>
> I felt good that our town's Latino and black populations were represented in the musical styles and were present in the audiences. This year these people were nowhere to be seen.

If we are to think of our town as a family, shouldn't we take a look at those family values our leaders keep talking about, and let our definition of "family" include
more than just 2.4 children and a dog?

Steel Town is also thriving and alive with the joys of the Christmas season. The
historic northern portions are lit with white monochromatic electric brilliance, while
the South Side displays multicolored garlands. The Christmas decor mirrors the seg-
regation of the culturally diverse populations. For the most part, the northern suburban and more affluent sections are comprised of monolingual residents. Residents of
the less affluent southern sectors of the city reflect diverse languages, cultures, and
religions.

Steel Town is a working-class community whose European settlers were Hugue-
nots, members of the Moravian Church of predominantly German ancestry. There is
a small Native American presence representing the Lenne Lanape, Delaware Indians,
comprised of only five citizens who can still speak the native language. Additional
culturally and linguistically diverse populations were attracted mainly as an out-
growth of the steel industry. In the past four decades, the major population growth
has been experienced by Latino/as, comprised mostly of native and mainland
Puerto Ricans and African Americans (see table 2.1).

Table 2.1. Population Growth in Steel Town, 1960–1990

	1960	1970	1980	1990
African Americans	1,014	1,363	1,572	2,080
Native American	na	na	na	na
Puerto Ricans	1,100	2,966	4,795	7,724
Other Hispanics	377	1,920	1,150	1,576
Total Hispanics	1,477	4,886	5,945	9,300
Total Minorities	2,491	6,249	7,514	11,380
Total Population	75,402	72,686	70,419	71,424

The religious and industrial strengths of the community are common attractions that have brought families to the region who experience differing economic
and political realities. The housing distribution, the individual occupations, the
houses of worship, and the schools attended are examples of how daily experiences
vary among families. Although there are exceptions, mainstream European groups
enjoy the benefits of home ownership, suburban lifestyles, and preferred and higher-
paying jobs. The Latino second-language speakers, on the other hand, comprise the
majority of the lower socioeconomic status group, participate in menial jobs, live in
modest or publicly subsidized housing, and comprise the less politically powerful in
the community. In spite of continued attempts by linguistically and culturally
diverse leaders to run for political office, the politicians of Steel Town are all mono-

lingual, monocultural, white residents. At this writing there are no residents of color serving on the school board, on the city council, or as elected officials of Steel Town.

A historical account of the community recounts the initial missionary intent of European settlers followed by an industrial-driven immigration. Bishop Nitschmann conducted missionary work among Indians in Georgia and was interested in establishing a "Negro School in Pennsylvania." The Six Nation Iroquois Confederacy is mentioned in the account. Bishop Nitschmann, however, is noted to be in charge of Indian Affairs and is regarded as the recognized founder of the community, along with fourteen other settlers (circa 1741). The settlers viewed their role on the five hundred-acre tract of land north of the river as preaching and the establishment of schools for the "hosts of neglected children and missions among the Indians" (Schwarz 1992, 8).

The Native Americans in the region today are neither counted nor officially recognized by the Commonwealth. I mention this because historical accounts make reference to an "Indian uprising" from 1756 to 1757. The Delaware Indians in the valley continue to face issues of equity, however, including linguistic human rights, land ownership, and ancestral needs, and do not appear in official government Census counts (Messinger 1995).

Purchase of 1,380 acres of farmland by the European settlers took place after the initial lease system was abolished. As the railroad and steel industries grew, so did the population of the South Side. In the 1860s and 1870s the primary immigrants were Irish and Germans. In 1880 the Irish comprised one-third of the city, followed by Slovaks, Hungarians, Ukrainians, Poles, and Slovenes (Windish). The first Italians arrived in 1895, the turn of the century saw the arrival of immigrants from Russia, Greece, Lithuania, and Croatia. Mexicans arrived after World War I. The first Puerto Ricans arrived in the 1930s, increasing substantially during World War II. Each ethnic group established its own churches and social organizations. The expectation was that each newly arriving group would pay its "dues": . . . In development common to other American cities, as each new wave of immigrants arrived, it would take the place of the immediate predecessors at the bottom of the social scale. (Schwarz 1992, 39).

The industrial elements of the community prospered. After Pearl Harbor all steel was earmarked for war production, with more manufactured steel produced in Steel Town than in any other place in the country. The current situation stands in sharp contrast to those years of high employment, with continued cutbacks and layoffs. The region has been forced to diversify its economic base and is in many ways in economic transition.

The bilingual families who were attracted to the community by the steel industry endured hardship. In spite of the fact that they were relegated to the most menial jobs, they continued to hope for a brighter and better future for their children. Dr. Sanchez, who was a participant in this study and a local professor born in Steel

Town, described his parents' struggle in the steel mill and in the community. His parents immigrated from Spain in the early 1950s.

DR. SANCHEZ: They came directly to Steel Town and my father got work at the steel-mill. They weren't allowed to hire blacks at the mill, so they hired Hispanics. My dad worked in the absolute worst part of the mill, the coke ovens. At that time they could not find people willing to stand the conditions, so they went to Mexico and brought people in box cars. They set up tents and lived in the fields right outside of town. It was extremely dangerous work. There has been a Latino community since the turn of the century. Spaniards came fleeing the Civil War, and migrants of Mexican and Puerto Rican descent came later. Some families have been here for many, many years. They were never accepted (by the rest of the community). They were basically ignored and employed for the low-level jobs. I remember both of my parents working two jobs. At the steel mill, the factories, and the schools it was clear that a segregated, racist system was in place.

The families in the community organized their lives and their children's lives with the prospect of a better future. The older generation Latino/as, *"los viejito/as"* (the seniors), the grandparents, arrived in Steel Town with optimism in their hearts and a willingness to "pay their dues" in order to benefit future generations. Don Jacinto, a sixty-seven-year-old senior and patriarch of the contemporary South Side, explains why the first generation of Latino/as learned to "swallow" mistreatment and intolerance:

DON JACINTO: When we first came here, times were hard, times were very hard. I have lived here in the South Side for over thirty five years now. I remember the night that the police rounded us up and took us to jail. Johnny, Laura's father, was with us, Don Rodrigo, and Gutierrez. We had *not* done anything, *aaannnyyy-thing!* But they told us that they didn't like our speaking in Spanish. The police and the peoples here have humiliated us in many, many ways. We put up with it. We put up with a lot. And you know why? Because we think it will help our children. We think it will help the future of our children. We thought that if we "swallowed" and put up with it, then it would be easier for our brothers. *Tragamos, y tragamos, y tragamos.* [We swallowed, and swallowed, and swallowed.] But I wonder now, if we did the right thing.

The sentiments expressed by Don Jacinto reflect the silencing of Latino voices in Steel Town. The regret he expressed for his continued silence is a result of more recent events. In January 1993 the local school board, at the school superintendent's urging, eliminated the local school district's bilingual education program in favor of an English-only curriculum. When Don Jacinto "wonders now, if we did the right thing," he expresses his view that the voices of the bilingual community and the bilingual children in opposition to this decision were eloquent, yet disregarded by the decision makers.

Individuals in positions of power in Steel Town have a history of effectively fore-closing Latino participation in the political and educational process. The main-stream residents, for the most part, view Latino/as as non threatening and as "good Hispanics." The definition of "good Hispanics" is a group of people who will "keep to themselves" and "cause no problems." A newly arrived, European American describes her experience:

MRS. READ: Our children attended the local public schools in California. Their experi-ences were positive and we were pleased with the district. We were as actively involved as our schedules permitted. The children thrived, so we never considered a private school. When I tried to register them here locally, however, I realized that my children would be exposed to a climate of racism. [This family has three adopted Spanish-speaking, Central American children.] I was informed that Hispanics in this community would be of no consequence and that I should not worry. "They stick to themselves," I was told. "They bother no one." I was shocked. I told Jerry [her husband] that our children would be harmed by such attitudes. There was no question as to how we should proceed. I still continue to be shocked by the racism of the area. Honestly, I have never seen anything like this.

Mrs. Read wanted to be supportive of public education and would have been an asset to the school, but after this experience the family opted to place their children in a local private school.

My visit with Latino senior citizens in the community center helps explain the coping strategies of the older Latino generation. A large sign at the top of a wall sums up the sentiment: "*Escuchar, Mirar, y Callar*" ("Listen, Look, and Be Quiet"). The strategy that this particular generation has internalized and passed on to the next generation is one of total passivity and subjugation. The roles of the oppressed and oppressors are well delineated and reflected in my observations of interactions at community celebrations, schools, work-places, and public services. At the annual banquet held in a spacious local establishment and sponsored by the largest Latino organization in Steel Town (October 1993), for example, the coveted awards indicat-ing service to the community were given to white politicians. Red-carpet treatment was afforded the Anglo guests from Steel Town, including seats of honor and seats closest to the invited speakers. The *respeto* afforded to the white politicians appeared unwarranted to me, when viewed by the Latino/as who described pain, hurt, oppression, discrimination, and humiliation.

As I listened to conversations among second-generation families at community meetings, silence continued to be encouraged as an intergenerational coping strategy. Elena, a young mother with two elementary school-aged children, is currently coping with the educational needs of her children:

DOÑA ELENA: El problema Hispano es uno de miedo. No sabemos nuestros derechos. Y si sabemos nuestros derechos no nos atrevemos. Si nos quejamos en la escuela puedes estar seguro que la policia va pasar por nuestra casa. Los ninos son los que sufren . . . y por ellos tenemos que evitar. [The Hispanic problem is one of fear. We do not know our rights. And if we know our rights we don't dare. If we complain at school, you can be sure that the police will come by our house. The children are the ones to suffer . . . and for their sake we must avoid (any problems).]

The rationale families give for "swallowing hard" and for maintaining the climate of silence is to benefit their children. The feeling seems to be that if the adults in the community are quiet, silent, and do not cause problems, their children's safety and well-being will be safeguarded. Putting children first, a child-centered orientation, is among the most commendable values families can impart. In this case, however, it seems like a well-intentioned but misguided effort. How does the ability to "swallow hard" affect the mental health of the parents? How does the climate of silence influence Latino/a children's self-esteem, self-confidence, and empowerment? How does the willingness to put up with indignities affect the future power of the younger generation? The families seem to feel that they are building a base for the future of their children. Is their silence and passivity enhancing the Anglo power base in the community?

Maritza gives her second-grade daughter advice (*consejo*) regarding how to behave and interact with Anglo Americans:

DOÑA MARITZA: Lo mejor que puedes hacer es quedarte callada! Trata a los gringos bien, que algun dia ellos te trataran bien a ti. Lo importante es que no causes problemas. Siempre calladita, bien, bien humilde, y ya tu veras. [The best thing you can do is to stay quiet! Treat the "gringos" well, and someday they will treat you well. What is important is that you cause no problems. Always quiet, very, very humble, and you will see.]

How does Maritza's daughter learn to negotiate between home and school contexts? The *consejo* Maritza imparts is of continued silence, with the hope that someday the mainstream society will treat her well. Families transferred their ability to influence and any inherent power to their oppressors readily and willingly. The conversations that I heard between parents and children did not include ways of advocating and enhancing the existing Latino power base.

Two Latino/a leaders in Steel Town recalled how particular experiences in the community affected them and their children. Dr. Rodriguez, an administrator in higher education, recalls experiences with police officers while Dr. Rivera, a local medical doctor, retells a friend's experience and an experience at the local hospital:

DR. RODRIGUEZ: All these years I have shared my anger with the boys . . . about how the system treats our people. I talk about discrimination, racism, and injustice. Each time a policeman has talked to me, however, they have seen a different mother! I can still hear them saying, "Why did you say, 'Yes, Sir' to him? Why didn't you speak up? You didn't do anything wrong. He pulled you over for no good reason." The boys were puzzled, and I am too. Why do I react as if I am scared for my life?

DR. RIVERA: I have a good friend [name] she works for [company]. She has two boys . . . and her oldest boy [name] has been looking for a job. We were actually discussing this not so long ago, about his experiences in this community and the school system. He was very bitter, he was extremely bitter. He is MexicanAmerican, second-generation, and the Anglo kids looked down on him . . . experiences such as dating a girl, the daughter of a realtor who was forbidden to see him because he's Mexican. He would be driving through a particular neighborhood, visiting a friend . . . and the police would stop, question him and ask him what he was doing in that neighborhood. The police also stop him because he fits the description of someone who has stolen a car . . . or whatever . . . even though he's by law a citizen. He was hurt and he's still very hurt!

Dr. Rivera also recalled personal experiences in the local hospital and the community as they related to issues of language:

DR. RIVERA: So Dr. Medina and I could be walking down the aisle in the hospital and we may choose to speak in Spanish between ourselves. So I received this complaint . . . The nurses were very angry, they were upset because we were speaking Spanish and they could not understand what we were saying. I could not understand that . . . It was a private conversation. When we were building [their office building] the workers made a comment about how unhappy they were . . . Medina and I were discussing something in Spanish because it's just the easiest language for us to use. One worker made it known that he would not talk to us personally . . . and raised his voice about "these people talking in Spanish." It took me by surprise. I didn't say anything. It's his problem, not mine. But I've had many experiences like that in which people feel threatened. . . . There's a paranoia about not being able to understand. The ultimate thing is that they want the culture to be integrated.

The *consejo* to remain silent and not cause trouble imparted by Latino/a elders within the community context is not helping alleviate similiar kinds of oppression reported by the adult informants in this study. The "swallowing hard" *consejo* appears to be a prevalent childrearing practice across the generations, but most specifically with the elders. One *abuelita* (grandmother) told me how she reinforces this advice by reminding her granddaughter that "Silence is more powerful than words." The questions remain: Will continued silence help future generations of Latino/a children cope in an increasingly complex society? Will the continuation of childrearing practices that encourage silence nurture a healthy, confident generation of Latino/as?

An article in the local paper (August 22, 1993) shows some alarming statistics in Steel Town and two interconnected communities. The suicide rates for local residents of this area outnumber those of the state and the rest of the nation. The article cites one city as having a 43 percent higher suicide rate than the state, the second with a 40 percent higher rate, and Steel Town with a slightly higher rate than the overall state rate of 1,192 suicides per 100,000 residents. The greater share of the suicides is implemented by older white males. These rates have not changed in the past decade in spite of improved mental health knowledge. What type of a social climate creates these disturbing statistics?

The German settlers who came to the area admire themselves for their tremendous work ethic. A companion to this attribute, however, has been the philosophy of "rugged individualism" that encourages a person to keep all emotions and feelings hidden. The thinking is that a person's suffering is his or her own, to be shared with no one. This stoic Pennsylvania (German) Dutch attitude is prevalent in the community, but may ultimately be harmful to the contemporary mental health needs of the group.

The sharing prevalent in extended family relationships and modeled by Latino families may prove useful to persons with a stoic attitude in light of such high suicide rates. Perhaps the Pennsylvania Dutch attitude could benefit and learn from the social relations modeled by ethnically diverse families. What wisdom might individualistic-driven societies gain from collaborative cultures? Will the doors of humanity and compassion ever open to meet the needs of children growing up in an increasingly complex society?

At this writing, it is evident that Steel Town continues to alienate its Latino residents in a multitude of ways. Continued city council and school board elections result in no Latino/a representation. The "good Hispanics" continue to be silenced in both the educational and political processes. How has the philosophy initiated by Don Jacinto's generation, the need to "swallow," perpetuated itself? The realities faced by culturally and linguistically resilient families have helped establish warm, helpful relations among themselves and with the whole community, but the issue of silence remains a questionable and largely misunderstood strategy for coping with challenges.

3

Success Stories

"Our Language is at the Heart of Our Culture"

The political climate and the popular media have tended to direct our thinking toward a particular worldview of language-minority populations. Instead of celebrating the positive attributes of linguistically and culturally diverse families, the focus of discussion has centered on problems, deficit perspectives, and stereotypical notions. Much of the literature has tended to "blame the victim," while the media continue to portray bilinguals as violent, criminal, low-achieving, and unemployed. Demographic data do show high poverty rates (U.S. Bureau of the Census 1991; Miranda 1991; National Puerto Rican Coalition 1992; Yzaquirre 1992), but data also show high job participation and working families who reflect core American family values. Our ability to disseminate accurate and realistic information about bilingual families is especially important for people who need to change their thinking and behavior. The successful aspects and positive attributes of bilingual families have been overlooked in a national climate that encourages linguistic repression.

In discussions reported elsewhere (Soto 1992a, b), I refer to needed directions in the field of bilingual/multicultural education research. Among these are the need to pursue the "successful aspects" of language-minority populations and the need for alternate research paradigms. The former refers to the need to move away from deficit perspectives in the literature that continue to "blame the victim," while the latter refers to broader, more comprehensive, and ultimately experimental research designs in the field. This study serves as a modest attempt to "walk the talk," if you will.

All language-minority families are success stories in light of resilience and an ability to succeed within oppressive community climates. I refer to the twelve interview participants as "success stories" because they were nominated by members of the bilingual community for their leadership skills and were described as "well respected in the community." I also believe the mainstream society would regard their accomplishments as successful. Families interviewed would often nominate additional families; some received multiple nominations, including Mrs. Escobar's family, Dr. Cintrón's family, Professor Diaz's family, and Mrs. Torres' family. All of the persons with "success stories" completed graduate levels of education, comprise upwardly mobile families, and actively advocate for their community. This part of the research portrays bilingual families in Steel Town who attained career and personal goals in spite of hostile educational climates.

The interviews revealed striking similarities in educational perceptions despite the informants' differing circumstances and professions. Two major areas helped establish a broad framework for the interviews: (1) the family's daily interactions with schools and (2) school and life experiences (see appendix D for sample grand tour questions). Early educational experiences and barriers that the participants faced while negotiating with schools and communities were evidenced in the interviews. During these interviews, the families often reflected upon formative educational experiences and the contemporary contributions of schools to their family life. Most of the participants were born in Puerto Rico; since their parents migrated to the mainland, the interviews reflected comparisons between mainland and island schools.

The families reflect diverse occupations and interests. Eight of the families reside in intact family households while two families have a single head of household. Ten of the participants are currently involved in raising school-aged children. Eight families send their children to private schools, and two families send their children to the local public schools. The informants ranged in age from thirty-two to forty-seven and have lived in Steel Town from five to thirty-seven years. All twelve families reside within the city limits or nearby suburbia. Nine families are home or property owners, living in settings that range from modest town houses to plush homes. As a rule, descriptions of their early childhood homes were in sharp contrast to their current situations.

Table 3.1 shows some of the similarities and diversity among the families.

Table 3.1. Bilingual Families Interviewed

Family	Occupation	Place of Birth	Years in Steel Town	Children at home
Mrs. Alvarado	Social Worker	Puerto Rico	13	One
Mrs. Peralta	Social Worker	Puerto Rico	37	Two
Mrs. Montero	Public School Admin.	Puerto Rico	25	One
Mrs. Sotomayor	Admin. Industry	Puerto Rico	9	Two
Dr. Sanchez	Higher Education Admin.	Steel Town	36	None
Mrs. Torres	Public School Admin.	New York	7	Four
Dr. Ortiz	Higher Education Admin.	Puerto Rico	12	None
Dr. Cintrón	Medical Doctor	Puerto Rico	23	Two
Dr. Felix	Psychologist	Puerto Rico	10	Four
Mrs. Escobar	Public School Admin.	Puerto Rico	27	One
Dr. Rodriguez	Higher Education Admin.	Puerto Rico	5	Two
Professor Diaz	Attorney	New York	8	Three

The families were well represented in the helping professions and indicated that their career goals were often tied to a strong commitment to bilingual families. The idea of "helping my people" was commonly repeated in the interviews. Mrs. Sotomayor's and Professor Diaz's homes were often the sites of modest social gatherings and informal meetings. During informal conversations, Dr. Cintrón was often the object of admiration because of his generosity to the Puerto Rican community, his economic standing, and his ability to live "among the rich white people."

During my stay in Steel Town, I observed nine families actively participating during the bilingual controversy in the community when the school board eliminated bilingual education, and during Spanish-speaking community activities such as the Puerto Rican Day parade, the summer picnic, the winter awards ball, the Community Council, and Christmas festivities. Families participating in the community council were among the most active advocates for bilingual education, having access to the media and politically powerful players in the community at large. As the families related the impact that educational institutions had on their lives, it was evident that they were successful despite the system, not because of it. Their experiences in mainland and island schools led to discussions both with me and among themselves about racism and inequitable treatment of language-minority children in the mainland schools.

The informants who participated in bilingual education programs on the mainland related positive experiences and attributed much of their success to bilingual education. Professor Diaz and Mrs. Torres, for example, indicated that bilingual education programs in New York City far surpassed any programs in Steel Town. The other participants described feelings of isolation when, as recently arriving migrants, they were placed in "sink or swim" submersion programs in the Commonwealth of Pennsylvania. Their memories of early educational experiences were often painful to recall. Several interviews led to tearful, passionate portrayals of uncaring and oppressive schools.

Raising Children Bilingually

When I analyzed the ethnographic interviews, I found repeated common themes. The first theme denoted the interviewees' desire to raise their own children bilingually. The families described a dialectical relationship between the home language and the home culture. As families faced the challenge of initiating a home learning environment capable of encouraging and enhancing linguistic and cultural learning, they described how they implemented a variety of approaches. The families with a background in education, for example, advocated a "one parent–one language" approach and initiated this bilingual approach at birth.

MRS. ESCOBAR: Both my husband and I are fully bilingual. We always wanted that for our children. . . . My mother was the one who took care of him [their son] for me while I worked, so she spoke to him in Spanish all the time and then Felipe and I decided that I would speak to him in English and he would speak to him in Spanish as well, just to reinforce what my mother was doing during the day with him. And that seemed to work out very well. He is seven years old now. . . . If I speak to him in Spanish and when he tries to answer me in English, I will say, "I spoke to you in Spanish, please answer me in Spanish."

DR. RODRIQUEZ: At home my father always spoke to us in Spanish and my mom always spoke to us in English. . . . My father was the reader, so there were tons of newspapers in the house all the time and magazines and they were both English and Spanish. Right from the very beginning . . . the music, the literature.

DR. CINTRÓN: You can have a child be bilingual. . . . You should have one of the parents speak to the child in one particular language and then the other should speak the other particular language.

The one parent–one language approach is supported by early case studies viewing early childhood bilingualism (McLaughlin 1984). In addition, studies conducted by Bain (1974) and Bain and Yu (1980) found that young children raised with the one person–one language approach outperformed monolingual and mixed bilingual children on four tasks involving verbal instructional strategies.

Other professionals I interviewed opted to "temporarily" sacrifice home language development with the hopes of assuring early English language proficiency and school acceptance of their child. One father, for example, began the one parent–one language approach but discontinued it and implemented an English-only approach when he felt that his children were not acquiring higher levels of English needed for the school's academically rigorous English-only curriculum. His children now have difficulty speaking to their grandparents, and he expresses considerable sadness at this loss of communication. It was evident that the children's mother appears limited in English proficiency. What impact the implementation of an English-only environment at home will have on the children's relationship with their mother can only be surmised.

Encouraging Cultural Pride

The need for children to be proud of their Puerto Rican heritage was also expressed repeatedly in the interviews. The participants viewed their parents as the source of their own cultural and ethnic pride. A genuine effort was made by families to ensure that their children were aware of cultural and historical accomplishments. Dr. Cintrón referred to the "cultural integrity of the family," while Mrs. Peralta fears the school's influence.

DR. CINTRON: There is a need to keep the cultural integrity of the family.

MRS. ESCOBAR: We go out of our way to speak to him about the positives of being Puerto Rican and the beauty of difference.

MRS. PERALTA: I can show Carlitos to be proud about the fact that he is Puerto Rican, but then he gets to the school and the teacher says that Puerto Ricans are bums.

The families also recalled gatherings filled with special traditions, sights, sounds, and tastes that were unique during their formative early childhood years. Such traditions helped the participants understand issues of language and culture in the informal and caring family setting. The intergenerational wisdom and values given by the family to its young children left a lasting impression on these adult informants. As children they developed in an increasingly complex society so that the traditional wisdom and knowledge helped them gain a strong sense of self.

Mrs. Torres' family still gathered around the kitchen table each year to prepare *pasteles* for the Christmas celebration. The division of labor included the youngest as well as the oldest child. Mrs. Torres' sister-in-law told stories that were elaborate, detailed, and humorous as she recalled her youth and her experiences as a newly arriving immigrant (Puerto Ricans obtained U.S. citizenship and access to the military draft as a result of the 1917 Jones Act). The descriptions of the people she met on the mainland included "less civilized" cultural comparisons to Puerto Rican behaviors she valued. The whole *pasteles*-making process took an entire leisurely day. As she told it, the grandmother was the organizer and the expert, while Mrs. Torres was charged with the more labor-intensive, hands-on activities. This collaborative cooking experience exemplified language learning and intergenerational cooperation. Children learned family histories and traditions gathered around the kitchen table in an informal setting.

A Supportive Family Climate

The "success stories" of the participants conveyed an environment of nurturance and a climate supportive of education provided by their parents. They described rich print environments, enriching family activities, and a high regard for educational personnel even when a personal sense of right dictated otherwise. Daily homework routines, in which children learned academic knowledge from parents and parents improved their own language proficiency from their children as teachers of English, were described. The respect accorded educators by the participating families was compared to the respect accorded Jesus, the Savior, to Christian families throughout the world.

PROFESSOR DIAZ: Education was a high priority to my father and to my mother. My
   father took us to the library and showed us how to walk to the library by
   ourselves. My sister and I came home with two, three, or four books (depending
   on the size of the books). Papi would ask us questions about what we read. He did
   not understand what we had read, but he wanted us to tell him something. He
   knew the value of an education. I continued to do this with my own daughter. I
   would take her to the library, I would read with her, I would teach her.
MRS. TORRES: There was a high-quality reverence toward education in my family.
   We were expected to look at the teacher and see Jesus. If you begin to think that
   your teachers need to be respected as much as Jesus, then you think that they
   know what to do, they know what is right, without any question.
MRS. MONTERO: My parents died when I was young. But speaking for my mother,
   education was very important. I always remember that she always wanted me to
   be the first in my class, to have the best grades and to be the first one in everything.

The idea of comparing a teacher to Jesus may help explain the amount of
respect some families accord educators. When teachers give advice to families, they
need to understand that families have placed them in authoritative positions of high
regard. Is the supportive educational climate families provide mirrored by the
schools? Are there questions that we should be raising regarding what constitutes
ethical teaching practices and ethical educational advice?

Indignation

A recurrent theme of indignation—personal pain coupled with anger—was also evidenced. The mainland schools were portrayed as environments that supported climates of oppression. A variety of experiences and issues were noted, with the most
salient being the lack of optimal knowledge on the part of school officials regarding
what constitutes best educational practices for bilingual children. Issues of assessment and teacher insensitivity reflected major areas of concern. In addition, the
families expressed concern about a "long history of miseducation of bilingual learners."

MRS. MONTERO: In elementary school [in Puerto Rico] I always liked school, I loved
   school. Going to school was a joy. I just loved it. I was always at the top of my
   class. I had lots and lots of friends. I was a very happy child in school. I wanted to
   be number one academically. I wanted to be number one within the volleyball
   team. I won the *pista y campo*—I always wanted to be first in everything.
      Then I came to the United States when I was in eighth grade. That was horrible!
   I went from being a very happy, popular girl to being a nobody in school. I was the
   only Hispanic. There were no blacks. I was so different from everybody else. I did

not understand English as it was spoken here. They thought I was somewhat retarded or LD. They did not know what I was but they knew that there was something wrong with me. So they decided to put me in Special Ed. . . . and I didn't want to go to school.

It was horrible, horrible, horrible. So I didn't finish the year. I went back to Puerto Rico, where I finished high school and I was able to go to college.

Mrs. Montero, a public school administrator, contrasted her educational experiences in Puerto Rico with those in the mainland schools. The mainland schools "decided to put me in Special Ed.," she recalls. The fault-finding mission of educational/psychological assessment was blinded to Mrs. Montero's strengths and gifts and those of language-minority children. Mrs. Montero, who is often described as a bright and articulate professional, faced the experience of misplacement in the public mainland schools. It becomes evident that as long as placement and assessment strategies continue to encourage deficit paradigms, positive attributes, including children's gifts and talents, will be missed. Professor Diaz described the contrast between home and school.

PROFESSOR DIAZ: The hallways were filthy, the bathrooms looked like a war zone, the smell of urine permeated the most unlikely places . . . yet our home was immaculate. My father used all kinds of analogies from the Bible. He taught us to forgive, but I remember the one time he reflected on the school's condition and stated, "Contra entonces nosotros estamos tan chavao como estaban los judios." The pain in my father's face convinced me that I wasn't going to be a victim of circumstances.

Professor Diaz recalls a comparison by his father from the Bible with contemporary conditions experienced by Puerto Rican children in schools. Jonathan Kozol, in *Savage Inequalities,* reports the disparity of schools in America just as Professor Diaz describes in his interview. It was apparent that his home life was a refuge from the conditions he experienced at school.

The Loss of Language and Culture

The families revealed interactions with school personnel that devalued their native language and culture. How schools initiate the process of language loss is of interest here as is the idea that schools are capable of initiating a systematic process that results in the loss of languages and cultures. Mrs. Escobar recalls how schools implemented an English-only climate.

MRS. ESCOBAR: They used to tell us. Now speak English, now you are in America
(even though Puerto Rico is a Commonwealth of the United States of America),
and the message that we got loud and clear was the fact that little value was placed
on our language and culture throughout my elementary education.

PROFESSOR ORTIZ: We were requested to speak more English at home or to only
stop speaking Spanish at home, and speak English for the sake of her [child]
learning the language. I tried to help them [school officials] understand.

PROFESSOR DIAZ: In school there was a negative reinforcement, but at home our
parents encouraged us to learn, so there was a positive reinforcement. There was a
point when neither my sister nor I wanted to speak Spanish at school or at home.
The school took away our language. It was too embarrassing. . . . If you spoke
Spanish they would make fun of you, so you didn't want to speak Spanish.

The idea that "the school took away our language" is repeated by language-
minority professionals (Barrerra 1992). The linguistic and cultural repression in
Steel Town and in the Commonwealth is a reminder of the Carlisle Indian school
experience—perhaps the most glaring example of how mainland schools implemented a systematic process of linguistic and cultural repression. More than a century ago children traveled from their homes and their loved ones to government-run
and missionary boarding schools to comply with the government's experiment to
assimilate over eight-thousand Native American children in schools like Carlisle.
The idea was to place children in boarding school environments in order to assimilate them into white America.

Richard Henry Pratt, director of the Carlisle school, subscribed to Darwinism
and Calvinism and held the notion that white European culture was superior.
Correspondence that Pratt received is housed at Yale University and reflects letters
from Native American parents begging for their children. Linda Witmer (1995),
author of the *Indian Industrial School,* views this type of assimilation as an experiment that failed. John Slonaker, at the U.S. Army Military History Institute in
Carlisle, indicates, "It was in our perspective today, a racist concept" (Cullen 1995,
G2). Is the philosophical paradigm of the *Carlisle school mentality* continuing to
drive existing educational practices by forcing children to learn and speak only
English in order to be assimilated?

Mrs. Peralta also compared her experiences in the mainland and island schools.
She said she felt devalued in the mainland schools, while in Puerto Rico she felt valued.

MRS. PERALTA: In Puerto Rico I had completed third grade *con honores* ["with
honors"]. I was used to being the highest-achieving student in a large urban
school. When I arrived in the States, they informed me that I had to repeat third
grade. I don't know how they made their decision because I was never tested or
interviewed . . . and neither were my parents. That was only my first taste of a
string of painful experiences in school.

The placement decisions for language-minority children included "being held back" or repeating a grade. This along with special education misplacement signaled the schools' inability to provide for the needs of language-minority children. How was placement decided since there was no evidence of testing or parental interviews? Did the child's ethnic surname or conversational language proficiency determine the school's decision? How much specific knowledge did schools obtain to determine language-minority children's abilities?

Discrimination in Schools

Discrimination was an integral part of the educational experiences portrayed by the interviewees. These experiences varied but were evident, regardless of socioeconomic background or language proficiency. In Steel Town, Mrs. Montero shared how being from her neighborhood affected her school experiences.

MRS. MONTERO: I felt discrimination, but the discrimination had less to do with being Latino or speaking Spanish. It had to do with coming from South Steel Town. One busload came from South Steel Town and we were all looked upon as the pits of the pits.

Mrs. Alvarado cried when she recalled the distinction between "negrita" and "nigger" as one of her earliest demeaning experiences in the mainland schools. In Puerto Rico "negrita" is used as a term of endearment by family members. Adults use the term lovingly with children, and husbands use the term lovingly with wives in Puerto Rico, but on the mainland it's a different story.

MRS. ALVARADO: All of a sudden some of the kids started calling me "nigger." I didn't know what that meant, at first but I was excited to think that I was making friends so fast. I felt the kids really liked me.

I have a brother who is seven years older who walked me to school so he could meet my new "friends". Finally he heard it one day and told me. "Nigger is not the same as negrita," he told me. I was crushed because I thought it was a nickname, a sign of friendship, not ridicule.

Dr. Rodriguez recalls a gatekeeping experience when students in her class were tested for gifted programs. Dr. Rodriguez and another student in the class were effectively foreclosed from the gifted program. They were not allowed to compete on the entrance examinations. This is how Dr. Rodriguez remembers the incident:

DR. RODRIGUEZ: I told my mother that my friends were being tested over and over. They never asked me if I wanted to take the tests. The teacher dispatched Rodney and me to the principal's office to wait for three whole days. There were no explanations given. Rodney and I sulked all day and kidded each other about our good fortune, but we were really quite hurt.

My mother thought I was being punished (thereby hiding information), so early one day, she rushed to the office to find out about my transgressions. My mother was told that the students in our class were being tested for gifted programs—with the notable exception of Rodney and yours truly (the only minority children in the class).

At the time, Dr. Rodriguez could not verbalize or distinguish between implicit and explicit signals. She did, however, experience feelings that signaled the oppressive climate and worldview permeating the school. Ways that children gain understandings within the school setting can be attributed to their perceptions and feelings of being welcome or unwelcome, appreciated or unappreciated, valued or devalued.

DR. RODRIGUEZ: I don't remember consciously, what was going on. I was a kid, because I didn't know what the issues were intellectually, but I could *feel* that we were not welcomed. We learned in school that there was such a thing as prejudice. People didn't like us because we were Puerto Ricans.

Nonfamily Mentors

The "success stories" reported the assistance of a mentor at the high school level who helped the participants recognize their worth by assisting with the mechanics of college applications and scholarships. Two informants revealed an additional mentor at the college level, while others noted the lack of minority peers in college.

MRS. MONTERO: I owe probably my college education to the nuns at [school] who saw I guess a spark in me and knew just how to help me do what I needed to do to go on to college. The counselor who was a nun was very directive in her approach, "Get these filled out. Tell your parents that they're for college. Bring them back to me tomorrow."

That is the same approach that I encourage counselors to use with our kids. Some people may think this is spoon feeding but for those of us who were first-generation kids going to college, our parents knew nothing about how to help us fill out financial aid forms or college application forms. You need to be a lawyer to do those things.

MRS ESCOBAR: I was in Dr. Ray Burke's program. Dr. Ray Burke was my mentor and was very open-minded and an inspiration. I definitely received many of the tools I needed to open doors for me professionally at Lorraine University. I obtained a good education. There was a sterile environment in terms of the entire graduate school. There were no people of color. I never met another Latino while I was there.

DR. ORTIZ: There was this one English teacher, Mrs. Smith, who would help me. She would hunt me down. She wouldn't let me get away with murder. And I appreciated that because she showed me that she cared.

Specific assistance with paperwork proved valuable to families who were sending children to college for the first time. The high expectations imparted by nonfamily mentors aided in encouraging feelings of worth and assuring students that their goals were attainable.

The emerging themes gleaned from the ethnographic interviews conducted with "successful bilingual families" can be summarized as follows:

(a) an expressed desire to raise children bilingually (Spanish/English)

(b) depictions of parents as a source of cultural and ethnic pride

(c) a caring home learning environment supportive of education

(d) a recurrent theme of indignation (personal pain coupled with anger) toward school personnel who revealed insensitivity, lack of knowledge, and a "long history of miseducation" of bilingual learners

(e) specific interactions with school personnel that devalued native languages and cultures

(f) discrimination in mainland schools as an integral part of the educational experiences,

(g) assistance by a nonfamily mentor at the high school (or college) level

With the notable exception of assistance obtained from a nonfamily mentor, a poem by Peter Spiro (1994, 146) entitled "Cause and Effect" helps describe the inequities experienced in the mainland schools by the informants :

> Cause you are poor
> you go to public school.
> Cause public school is free
> you get a lousy education.
> Cause you get a lousy education
> you are uneducated.

Cause you are uneducated
you are treated with contempt.
Cause you are treated with contempt
you are contemptuous of others.

How long will language-minority children face disparity in their educational experiences? Who stands to benefit? Will the poet's words, "Cause you are treated with contempt, you are contemptuous of others," permeate the hearts and minds of children?

Consejos for Schools

The bilingual families provided advice (*consejos*) that can assist schools. The families articulated the need for schools to move away from paradigms of shame to paradigms of compassion. Overcoming an oppressive climate that devalues the language and culture of the home was articulated. When the participants were asked, "What advice do you have for schools?" the following themes emerged.

First, provide access to quality programs. Families envisioned "quality programs" as programs where children's linguistic and cultural gifts are valued; where expectations are high; where academic learning is the norm; where humanistic and democratic approaches are implemented; where language-minority children are well represented in gifted programs; where leaders are created; where teachers care about the children; where the classrooms are clean and brimming with colorful materials; where children learn about technology; where creativity is appreciated; where communication between school and family takes place; where problem solving is evident; where all children experience a world of equity and justice. Families called for "quality programs" for bilingual children, the same kind of programs that children of privileged America have.

Second, implement programs capable of preserving home languages and cultures. This advice presents the need for schools in America to implement programs that maintain, extend, and enrich the gifts and talents children bring to the schoolhouse door. Subtractive educational paradigms that rob languages and cultures are proving costly to children and families.

Third, integrate caring and humanistic approaches. Early painful educational experiences led the "success stories" to conclude that bilingual children find it difficult to overcome oppressive educational climates. Data show their concerns were warranted since the participants made it, despite the system and not because of it.

Fourth, accept the fact that institutions of learning are not the only knowledge brokers. There is a need for schools to become respectful of the knowledge and wisdom families can impart. The research-based knowledge and expertise these professional families tried to offer to schools were met with resistance.

Fifth, model ways of encouraging linguistic and cultural integrity. This advice places leadership responsibilities on schools as agents of a democratic nation. Does a nation founded on principles of justice and equity need schools that reflect these values? What knowledge and curricular innovations can schools implement to promote these ideals?

Sixth, initiate mentoring relationships. The mentoring roles described by the families were often quite simple and mechanical in nature. Helping students with college applications was one piece of this advice. In addition, "ways of relating" with children that indicate high expectations and persistence proved valuable for these informants.

Seventh, interact and communicate in ways that value the attributes of bilingual families. If children see that the adults in their learning environment value the language and culture of their homes, it stands to reason that they will gain pride in the attributes of their families. The human relations and communicative patterns children observe in the "worlds of childhood" can have a long-lasting impact on how they regard themselves, their family, and their nation.

Finally, provide ethical and knowledgeable advice. Is it ethical for schools to encourage families to speak only English at home? Is it ethical for schools to devalue children's home language and culture? Are schools knowledgeable about what constitutes optimal practices for language-minority learners? The families interviewed depicted mainland schools as neither knowledgeable nor ethical on matters affecting the daily educational realities of bilingual children.

The interviewees described educational climates as having a continuum of oppressive practices. The experiences of the participants in the mainland public schools were among the most oppressive and painful to recall. These environments were reminiscent of the Carlisle school mentality and Jonathan Kozol's "savage inequalities." The overriding issue stemmed from the immersion in school settings that implicitly or explicitly condoned linguistic repression and racism. The informants described indignation, anger, and pain. They described discriminatory gatekeeping incidents. The informants felt unappreciated, disregarded, and worthless. The optimistic, caring home environment was a sharp contrast to the impersonal, oppressive school setting they experienced.

Schools reflecting a more empowering climate valued the family's home language and culture. Often these schools were private parochial schools or schools in Puerto Rico. The teachers either reflected the language and culture of the families or valued linguistic and cultural attributes. These schools were places that imparted high expectations and feelings of worth.

I observed a common attribute of active community participation by the "success stories." The families emphasized the importance of "giving back" to the bilingual community. These professionals often provided in-kind services. Dr. Cintrón initiated a clinic for poor children; Mrs. Escobar devotes time to a local Spanish-speaking organization; Professor Diaz actively represents families in their struggle to find a quality education for their children; and Mrs. Torres is president of a local community service. Each family helps shed light on the needs of Steel Town by modeling a caring curriculum for their nuclear family and for the community.

The families I met for these interviews were adults "who made it" despite oppressive educational climates. Their advice coupled with our existing bilingual education research can help guide schools in ensuring the educational success of language-minority children.

4

Early Schooling

"En Esta Escuela No Se Habla Español"

The formative early school experiences young children attain can have a far-reaching impact on their adulthood years (Schweinhart 1994). The literature viewing optimal educational practices for bilingual young learners continues to emphasize the importance of maintaining home languages and cultures (Collier 1992; Cummins 1979, 1989, 1994; Skutnabb-Kangas 1989; Soto 1993; Wong Fillmore 1992). Young children who are socialized with a strong knowledge base in the language and culture of their family are enriched in at least two ways. First, young children obtain the intergenerational wisdom that loving families impart as a part of the childrearing process. The intergenerational wisdom families provide includes stories and traditions that can help children understand the importance of sharing and caring. Second, young children robed in cultural and linguistic knowledge attain a healthy sense of self and family pride. The proliferation of subtractive early childhood English-immersion programs in America is inconsistent with the existing research knowledge base.

In the South Side of Steel Town, like so many other cities across America, the early school day hours are teeming with traffic, pedestrians, and business acitivity. The school bus drivers make their appointed rounds and pick children up at the designated areas. Latino/a parents and young children can be seen walking toward the local elementary school and toward the bus stops. Margarita was six years old and a first-grader, when I met her . She expected to walk to her neighborhood school with her mother and baby brother, but this year she and a group of Latino/a children were being bused to a suburban school. None of the suburban children were to be bused to the South Side schools. The busing issue created divisiveness in the community centering on issues of equity and the neighborhood school concept (see chapter 5).

Margarita had attended the first newly assigned school for several weeks. The school board's plan included a second reassignment and busing to a subsequent school the following year. Margarita lived with her mother, father, grandmother, and younger brother in a second-story apartment on the South Side. She spent much of her time with her family helping care for the baby and doing some light chores. The family walked to church on a weekly basis, visited neighbors occasionally, walked to the local library during the summer months, and shopped at the local *bodega*. Her father spent the week working in whatever seasonal jobs he could find, as he continued to search for a steady job. Mr. Serra would come home on weekends to see his family. The family lived in the community for almost two years.

The curriculum of the Steel Town elementary school Margarita was attending included English-only instruction. In the classroom, on the playground, and in all activities the children were expected to speak only English. Margarita told me that this experience was difficult, especially during reading time. Occasionally the teacher would work with her in ways that she considered quite humorous. "Table, chair, green, window, floor, up, down!" Margarita laughed as she imitated a loud voice of a teacher intent on rote memorization. She told me she felt sorry for the teacher, who seemed frustrated and at a loss for ways of teaching the second-language learners. She also said the teacher never hugged her and never smiled at her. Her teacher comes from a Pennsylvania Dutch background, whose cultural difference includes a strong custom of nonverbal expressions of affection and rare physical closeness. Margarita seemed frightened by a teacher who rarely smiled and ignored her much of the time, her mother indicated.

"En esta escuela no se habla español!" (In this school no Spanish is to be spoken) was the message Margarita wanted to share, but it seemed as if the English-only policy was but the tip of the iceberg. Margarita and her peers were experiencing oppressive and subtractive educational policies. The "English acquisition" program being implemented in Steel Town has meant that all activities and all communication are English-only (see appendixes). The bilingual program in Steel Town was initiated in 1971 with the hiring of its first bilingual educator, Mrs. Martinez. The modest pioneering program provided English as a second language, transitional bilingual education, and companion native-language instruction for newly arriving Spanish and Portuguese speakers. Controversy ensued when federal monies were obtained for the program and the school district attempted to refuse these monies; The Commonwealth's State Department of Education intervened on behalf of the children. Mrs. Martinez also appealed to the State Department and received assistance with regard to the overrepresentation of children limited in English proficiency in special education classes.

The elementary program was expanded in 1977 when self-contained bilingual education classes were initiated in Spanish and English for students. This program had two phases: the bilingual, which used native-language instruction, and the transitional, which used mostly English for instruction. By the mid-1980s any native-language instruction was eliminated from the high school. In 1988 the school administration recommended the reconfiguration of bilingual education into two elementary schools. The kindergarten to second-grade students were sent to one school while the third- to fifth-grade students were placed in a second school. At this time the program began to evolve into a three-phase program for the elementary school children. In 1992 the middle school bilingual program included two middle school sites. The program responded to the bilingual demographic changes which included an increase from 6.6 percent of the school district enrollment in 1971 to 21 percent of the enrollment in 1992.

In 1992 the bilingual program was providing services for 1,168 limited English proficient learners who represented twenty different languages. Spanish was the home language of 94 percent of the students. The office that coordinated the program relied on standardized assessment instruments and family interviews to make decisions about the student's language proficiency, placement into the various phases of the program, and the exit criteria into the mainstream English-only classrooms. The elementary transitional bilingual education program consisted of three basic phases: (1) the primary language instruction, (2) the sheltered English instruction, and (3) mainstream classroom placement with English for Speakers of Other Languages (ESOL) support. All students obtained English language instruction, including the primary language students who participated in ESOL. The program's coordinator attempted to maintain ESOL support for learners at least one to two years prior to complete mainstreaming. The English language proficiency of the individual student drove the placement, so that not all learners proceeded though all the phases of the program. An early exit into mainstream English-speaking classrooms was encouraged by the school administration. The high school program was largely English-only, although at one point in the history of the program an ESOL program had been available.

In 1991 the school district superintendent appointed a team of professionals and community members to examine the bilingual program and make recommendations for its improvement. The standardized achievement test scores and interviews with parents showed the success of the elementary school program. There was concern about the high school dropout rates for Latino/a students. The committee recommended minor changes in the program and expected that their suggestions would be adopted. (See Bilingual Program Recommendations, submitted by the Bilingual Committee, appendix A.) Instead, in the fall of 1992 the superintendent announced that he would recommend the termination of the program because, he asserted, it segregated Latino/a students. The superintendent recommended a program design that would immerse the students in an English-only curriculum regardless of their level of communication in English. (See Superintendent's Response to Bilingual Committees's Report, appendix B.) He indicated that support would be provided so that the program would not violate the *Lau v. Nichols* 1974 Supreme Court decision. In 1993 the board voted 4 to 3 to eliminate the program while community leaders filed a suit with the Office of Civil Rights.

After the elimination of the bilingual education program the district implemented an English-only program. When Margarita and her peers indicated "En esta escuela no se habla Español" (In this school no Spanish is to be spoken). It became clear that children's languages and cultures were not celebrated by the Steel Town school district. Additional evidence (see English Acquisition Plan, BASD, 1993, in appendix C) contradicts decades of educational research and indicates the intent to eliminate diverse languages and cultures in order to implement a homogenous English-only curriculum. Where is the ESOL special component? How does a buddy system help language-minority learners? Where are the assessment components for placement and academic achievement? How does the school know that the material is comprehensible to learners? What specialized training have teachers received in order to meet the needs of second-language speakers? Has the school's role in providing a climate of disregard for children's home language and culture translated into issues of power and status? Has the assimilationist Carlisle school mentality forced children to view the language and culture of their families as less than valued? How are children coping academically and emotionally in the immersion program?

The impact of subtractive (Lambert 1975) programs that rob children of their language and culture has been well documented (Arenas 1980; Cummins 1984; Garcia 1983; Hakuta 1986; Krashen & Biber 1988; Peal & Lambert 1962; Skutnabb-Kangas 1989; Soto 1993; Trueba 1987; Wong Fillmore & Valadez 1985; Wong Fillmore 1991). It is a concern to families and to professionals throughout America that our nation may already be reaping the seeds of subtractive programs. The early educational experiences children receive can either build a strong base for future success or rob them of future possibilities.

Prior to conducting the "success stories" interviews I conducted informal interviews to practice and pilot the ethnographic format. The participants were parents of young children. The pilot interviews further justified Margarita's concerns and document a history of miseducation and educational abuse in Steel Town. The Carlise school mentality has been alive and well for at least two generations. Each of the four mothers interviewed indicated raising young children, residing in the local community, and working at least part-time. Their educational attainments ranged from not having completed high school to having earned one undergraduate degree. These interviews also initiate discussion about the childrearing practices among families with diverse educational backgrounds. Experiences varied but there were commonalties in childrearing practices and a desire for a more equitable future for Latino/a children.

Antonia was born in Puerto Rico, educated in New York City, and works as a counselor at a local community church-based center. Her contribution to the interview process was brief, but the following excerpt reflects her experiences in a New York City bilingual school.

DoÑA ANTONIA: My name is Antonia, and I was born in Salinas, Puerto Rico, which is in the south of the island. I went to kindergarten there and I came here to the United States in 1973; I started here [New York City schools] in the first grade. I felt comfortable because it was a bilingual school. My experiences in general were positive. I never felt the conflict between the people or the languages. Most of the people I was with were Hispanic so I never had the conflict which I understand a lot of the students (in Steel Town) have. Right now they are in the bilingual program and it's incredible the conflicts they have.

Lori was born in Steel Town, is a high school dropout (pushout), recently lived in Puerto Rico, and works for a local church. Lori did not attend Steel Town's bilingual education program because her parents refused permission.

DoÑa Lori: My name is Lori with an "i," but they take a look at me and they say, Okay, Laura. I was born and raised here in Steel Town, and I had no bilingual education at all. I was the third child so I must have known some English. Most of the kids in my class were Anglo. I went all the way to twelfth grade and dropped out at twelfth. I think I was in fifth grade when bilingual was started. They came to our home and wanted me to join the class, to put all of us in the bilingual program. That we needed our Spanish 'cause we're Hispanic, and my mom and father didn't want it. We just spoke Spanish mostly to my father and my grandmother. My family learned to speak English. I had trouble with my daughter cause my daughter went to a Puerto Rican school and I'm dealing with both languages both over there and over here and it's complicated.

Juana is a member of a family who recently joined the Steel Town community. She was born in New York City, experienced busing, and works with an after-school tutoring program sponsored by a local church. She compared language-minority children to invisible shadows.

DoÑa Juana: I was born in Bellevue Hospital in New York. I've been here just a few months. The public schools were great. My father used to say, "You speak Spanish when you are in the house. English stays out the door." And it was always like that. I can understand, alright the government doesn't have enough money, but you can't give up on us. You cannot give up on tomorrow's future, 'cause then we're doomed. I mean I want to be a little old lady walking down the street, and I want to feel secure, but if we give up on today's kids. They know it. They're saying it. "Who cares?" I just didn't feel like going to school, I didn't want to go to school anymore. It was the first year in high school, there was a lot of racial tension. We were being bused into a white neighborhood. I'm not going to say Anglo because to say Anglo that means nothing. We were being bused into a white neighbor hood. You know if I would keep my mouth shut and walk through the neighbor hood, they would never know. Then you see another shadow go by . . . and there goes the kid. We didn't have the opportunity to be heard as kids. They are pushing the kids to grow up too fast.

Luz has lived in Steel Town for over twenty years, completed a high school GED diploma recently, and works for a local church. She shared the abuse she experienced in school.

DOÑA LUZ: They changed my name to Lucy. They couldn't pronounce the "z" in Luz. I used to get whacks on my head for not spelling my name the way they wanted it spelled. After all, they would say, You're an American. But the next person would say, You are Puerto Rican. The system is failing the kids, and it's not just one child.

Why go to a PTA meeting? They send you letters that say your kid is doing bad . . . then they tell you at the meeting your child is doing real well.

"I guess we made a mistake with another kid." Well they either don't have a clue of what they are doing, or they are prejudiced.

These initial interviews with mothers uncovered alarming methods schools used to silence bilinguals, including physical abuse (whacks on the head). The pain and humiliation these mothers shared have created a climate reflecting educational paradigms of shame. These mothers ascribed to a language learning approach for their children that mirrored the assimilationist perspective reflected by the larger community. Ultimately messages to conform have cumulative and the desired long-term consequences sought by the oppressors. The messages Lori and Juana received were of disdain, ultimately devaluing their home language and culture. The physical representation of the whacks in the head is an example of power of the most cohersive and abusive type: the Carlisle school mentality.

The "success stories" also relayed the types of English-only advice schools imparted during early schooling:

MRS. SOTOMAYER: The school told us last year he [her son] shouldn't read in Spanish, that we should make him read only in English. I would like for him to read and write in both languages, but the school knows more about teaching than I know. I am not of that background at all. José did not like it at all. He was mad and nasty and told me he thought the teacher was dumb. He didn't fight about it though; he knows you must obey the teacher.

The advice schools are imparting to families is unethical, in light of the fact that families trust educators to have the necessary wisdom and knowledge about what constitutes optimal practices for educating young children. The instructions provided to parents by educators may be followed religiously, as if it were the law of the land. The amount of trust and respect bilingual families have placed on educators has been largely unappreciated and, in many cases, unwarranted.

DR. ORTIZ: We were requested to speak more English at home or only stop speaking Spanish at home, and speak English for the sake of her [his daughter] learning the language. I tried to help them understand that she's been here for two years. I mentioned to the teacher that research shows that it usually takes about seven years to acquire the language and that the transitions are not always smooth. There is a tremendous amount of conceptual thinking that takes place. It was almost devastating. She got really turned off about school. She would avoid sitting down and doing any [school] work at all. I think that the tensions in the house just kind of peaked because here's Eva who in Puerto Rico was a very bright student and was working very well. Educators need to understand that language development can have an intense impact on any child.

Dr. Ortiz has attempted to educate personnel working with his child, but to no avail. This father is more knowledgeable about the research evidence than the school personnel. The research he cites refers to Cummins (1979), who relays the need for threshold levels of native language as a facilitator for second-language learning. In other words, higher levels of home language (e.g., Spanish) actually facilitate second-language learning (e.g., English). Cummins (1989) has also helped explain the distinction between social conversational language skills and the more complex cognitive academic skills. This distinction is important because speakers of second languages acquire the social surface fluency skills prior to the deeper, more complex conceptual curricular demands. Academic decisions about children's placement, instructional strategies, and assessment need to take into account the distinction between social and academic language proficiency.

The literature shows that large numbers of young bilingual children have been misplaced and misdiagnosed by schools. Ortiz and Yates' (1983) Texas study cites 300 percent overrepresentation of Hispanic students in the learning disabled category; Ruiz, Figueroa, Rueda, and Beaumont indicate that Hispanic children continue to enter the special education process under suspect circumstances (1992, 350). Mrs. Montero was among the statistics when she shared how she had been tested in English and identified as "mentally retarded" by school personnel. The fact that her vita shows two master's degrees and many educational accomplishments implies that gifted placement may have been far more appropriate.

Mrs. Montero shared the need for disseminating information to parents about how to best communicate with mainland schools. Bilingual parents oftentimes come from environments where teachers are revered. In some cultures it is impolite and rude to question the teacher's authority. The aura of respect accorded educators translates into not questioning the decision-making process. José Sotomajor's reaction to the teacher's advice exemplifies the issue of total and unquestioning respect. There is a need to communicate to parents their legal rights as well as the value of educational assertiveness on behalf of children.

Mrs. Peralta is a social worker in the community, with two young children in the local school. She relayed how issues of language, culture, and power have been an integral part of her own experiences.

MRS. PERALTA: I was dealing with a lot of teachers and administrators whose goal was mostly to wipe out the children from school, instead of learning more about them and their life experiences. It was difficult to fight the system. You are seeing many students, many human beings. . . . If the teacher doesn't do something, then we are not making a difference in their life. The teacher and the administrators, they do not know how to handle the background, how to positively use the experience that these children already have. The schools are not taking into consideration that they are serving children that are human beings. It is because we are Puerto Rican. The humbleness, the humbleness, the humbleness itself is abusive from our Indian roots. We delegate to others . . . we think that others are superior and have the knowledge.

The education process has to start from the experience and background of the children. Our people are losing interest because of our language and thinking that these teachers are superior. I think a good approach is to open the door to the parents . . . to see the teachers in the community. . . . Being raised in Puerto Rico, the teacher's image is something that is different here. I see the teachers here, afraid of the Puerto Ricans, afraid of the blacks, afraid of everybody. . . . Education is not effective because of all the biases.

Have you been to a welfare office? Oh my God! The way people are treated. Its as if you are an object a thing; it's like what happens in the school system. . . . the learning atmosphere does not promote the learning experience. . . . the atmosphere is not good. I'm an educated mother, and sometimes its hard for me to go to the school because my native language is not English. As soon as they hear the accent they relate the accent to intellectuality. Not all the parents have the education that we have and not all the parents have studied like we have. My self-esteem was strong. I was ready to come to Pennsylvania . . . but you know it's not easy.

Our people believe that the teacher has the *razon,* that you cannot question their decision. A child for me is the most important thing, my biggest investment in life. . . . It's sad to think that somebody can mess them up with a nonverbal gesture. Our children can sense it. Carlitos asks, Mommy, what happened to her, she's kind of mad? Or, Mommy, what happened with them, don't they like us? These little incidents happen on a daily basis . . . and if you're not strong . . . I know that the home has the responsibility for starting the child's education, but with the examples and attitudes they are finding in school . . . our education is not being reinforced. The school superintendent has been telling the newspaper that schools don't have to validate anybody's culture. What kind of an education does he have? He has never read Paulo Freire, who stated that the education has to be meaning-ful, has to start from the child's experiences in order to be pertinent and meaning-ful and effective. I don't know where he got his pedagogy training. . . . Every program, every institution, every agency in the country is an expression of the philosophy and the values of the country.

Mrs. Peralta's educational background, her knowledge about Paulo Freire, her experiences as a social worker, her knowledge about the Puerto Rican language and culture (comprising 25 percent of the local school district), and her experiences as a parent demonstrate a potentially valuable asset for this school district. Yet it is evident that she has felt overwhelmed and has found it hard to fight the system. Her frustration is evident, as is her concern for the manner in which the existing school climate is impacting her two young children.

The provisions classroom teachers made for students determined much of what participants experienced. Mrs. Alvarado recalled her painful early childhood experiences, including the notion of an assigned buddy.

MRS. ALVARADO: Mrs. Kaswitsy gave me a "friend" to serve as my leader and to help me some. I don't think Sarah was very happy about having to stay with me all day. She asked me one day if I was a Negro. She didn't seem to know what to make of me.

Mrs. Alvarado cried when she told additional early school experiences. "All through elementary school I had problems with racial discrimination," she stated. She goes on to describe her perception of the early educational needs of language-minority learners, including the teacher's role.

Caring is where it is at. . . . Someone has to show they care and early, early on. I am not at all sure that you can develop *ganas* at twelve or fourteen, or even nine or ten. It starts in the preschool. . . . It's scary to see the average Latino kid lives in projects, has no self-esteem . . . and when they do achieve something, they don't give themselves credit for it. God only knows what to do with teens who are so bitter, so angry. We can't make parents demonstrate interest in their children's learning. The reasons they aren't involved are too complicated to make a difference in most cases before the child is well on the way to disaster. I'm afraid its up to your teachers, and then only if they can get them at two or three or four, before irreparable damage to their self-esteem occurs. The big problem will be finding those teachers who have the knowledge and the energy to give that much to the kids. The difference they make is that of (saving) a life. That is pretty heavy, but the reality.

The "success stories" informants shared their notion of additive linguistic and cultural childrearing practices. The families integrated linguistic and cultural experiences at home and at school. Every attempt was made to affirm and reinforce cultural pride at home and, whenever possible, at school.

Mrs. Escobar described how she shared information with her son's teacher.

MRS. ESCOBAR: We go out of our way to speak to him about the positives of being Puerto Rican and the beauty of difference. He was about five when he started noticing that at his buddy's house they ate different food than we did. And we said, Well, isn't that exciting. Yeah, they don't eat rice and beans, Mommy! No, they don't make rice the way we do, but that's because we're lucky. We're Puerto Rican and Puerto Ricans make rice this way, isn't that wonderful. So I have worked very hard in terms of enhancing his self-esteem. We have an annual Puerto Rican parade . . . so there he is waving the Puerto Rican flag and I explained to him that some people have difficulty with people who speak other languages. Why Mommy? It's neat because I think he will deal with bilingualism from an ego strength point. I make it a point to make a presentation to his classmates on Puerto Rico. I've always been invited and he sits down with me and helps me. We share our culture with the class. We bring in instruments and show the children how to play them. We bring in our talk about our African influence, our Spanish influence, and our Indian influence. I usually make rice pudding Puerto Rican style and it is usually a very nice affair. And that also helps to empower him and he feels good about sharing the culture. One of the first things that I had to deal with was the fact that our name has an accent. So when he was in kindergarten and he was learning how to write his name and I'd say, Honey, your name has an accent and it goes here. So he came home one day and he said, Mommy, the teacher said that I should not put that little stick on top of my name. I sat down to write the teacher a letter telling her that the accent was as much a part of the letters in his name as one of the letters, that we are Latinos and that it had a different pronunciation if the accent was not there, so would you please see to it that he does put the accent every time he writes it. Well, they made an effort and even sent me a letter at home telling me to put an accent on my own name.

The families, regardless of socioeconomic status or educational levels, all voiced concern about the educational state of the art in schools, for young bilingual children. Mrs. Torres, a mother of four children, echoes this sentiment.

Mrs. Torres: We're not only failing the kids, we're failing the family, we're failing the parents, and we're failing our community. And when you put all of that together, we're failing this country. If our educational system is as poor as it is now, in another ten or twenty years when these kids are the ones that are going to be in power, and they're going to be the ones in leadership positions in the country, what kind of a country are we going to have? Its scary. We're not giving the kids the tools and we're not preparing them to run this country.

Professor Diaz noted his concern with the local public school in particular. He relates his view of the school district as arrogant and connects this attitude to issues of self worth and to the respect afforded educators by language minority families.

PROFESSOR DIAZ: This school district is very arrogant; they think that professionally they have all the answers. They do not look at the research on bilingual education that has come up in the last few years, they don't value it, they don't value our people's ethnicity. . . . Kids lose their self-esteem, or the self-esteem is taken away from them. . . . Here they use the assembly line approach in education which is reflective of the nineteenth century. This district needs to move to a school based management, participatory decision making, making sure the supplies are equal. The supplies in the North Side schools are a lot better than the South Side schools. More supplies, more plentiful supplies with the more experienced teachers in the North Side, and the least experienced teachers in the South Side. Parents are not taught what their educational rights are in this district. Parents are not parents— especially the Latino parents because of our culture. We tend to empower the teachers and the school system more than we should, because we say, "Ellos son los professionales, y que soy yo?" [They are the professionals, and what am I?]. We don't give ourselves enough credit.

The feelings portrayed by mothers with educational attainments ranging from undergraduate degrees to less than high school, reflected helplessness, frustration, anger, and a general climate of futility. The mothers expressed a desire to view their children functioning and succeeding within the educational context and the society at large. They view the current local educational system as failing not just one child but all children. They expressed a desire for teachers and schools who can under-stand the needs of young bilingual children. Their perceptions of the local program in the Steel Town schools indicate a view of a compensatory model of bilingual edu-cation that labels their children. The school's understanding of what bilingual edu-cation is, what the research findings indicate, and the diversity of bilingual programs is limited.

The mothers and one father with higher educational attainments ("success sto-ries") indicate an understanding of the bilingual education research, incorporate enriching linguistic and cultural learning experiences at home and at school, and view the local educational institutions as arrogant and failing children (and the nation). The families voiced the need for schools to be more knowledgeable about the educational needs of young language-minority children.

What can we learn from the bilingual families' early schooling? Advice for par-ents can be summarized as follows: obtain knowledge and communicative strategies that will be heard and acted on by schools. Advice for schools includes gain cultural-ly responsive and linguistically respectful knowledge as well as caring and best-prac-tices strategies that will enhance the educational learning environments of young children. Bilingual families envision the need for educational institutions to move away from paradigms of shame to paradigms of compassion.

Brendtro, Brokenleg, and Van Bockern (1990) refer to the hazards faced by children in contemporary society. They discuss the unfriendly school as a place that fosters discouragement and a climate of futility. Margarita and the families I interviewed shared experiences that paint a disturbing picture of the Steel Town schools. The schools are not only unfriendly, but are also creating oppresive and abusive climates of futility.

5

Agueybana Families

"Sit Down and Shut Up"

Cajigas, the Puerto Rican artist, designed a lithograph entitled *Agueybana*. It depicts a chieftain whose image imparts a sense of endurance and tolerance. Like the powerful image of this native leader, the bilingual families of Steel Town have been dressed in native courage and wisdom. Issues of oppression, intolerance, and racism have been evidenced in the community and it's schools for decades.

The "quiet ones," the "good Hispanics," showed solidarity as they organized themselves peacefully on behalf of their children's educational needs. The contrast between the school's intent to implement an English-only curriculum and the families' requests for bilingual education were evidenced in meetings with school officials. This chapter shows the *Agueybana* families struggling for voice.

Community Meeting

On the evening of March 11, 1992, the local community center was brimming with activity. Over 140 Spanish-speaking parents packed the small meeting room in the center. Whispered conversations, the signing of petitions, and flyers filled the room with excitement, optimism, and the feeling that it was possible for members of the community to have their voices heard. Representatives of the local school board and the school district superintendent were slated to speak about issues that would impact the South Side children. The panel members, comprised of the school district superintendent, selected school board members, and a school building principal, were all white. The translator who narrated the conversations for the Spanish-speaking parents and the coordinator of bilingual education were both Puerto Ricans. The parents and the community members were mostly Latino/a, with a few Anglo and African American parents.

The meeting's agenda, although not clear, included discussion by the school board regarding busing Latino/a children. Local newspaper reporters were present to record the events. The anticipation that the quiet and good Hispanics were about to speak up appeared to be unprecedented.

The audience was informed that the school district's plan would affect the long-term needs of the two elementary schools where Latino/a children attended.

Apparently at a previous school board meeting, unbeknown to the families, decisions were made as to how groups of children would be moved among the various elementary schools. The speakers indicated that children from one school would first attend a second school, and, at a later date, a third school.

Don Jacinto was the first to speak after the traditional introductions and the (not so clear) explanations about the purpose of this meeting by the school board:

DON JACINTO: I have lived in the South Side for over thirty-five years. I have seen what has taken place here. Why are you busing our children? Can you tell us about the study you sent in 1989? What was the overpopulation? What were the numbers for the Stony Garden School [referred to as the country club school]? In 1989, weren't there over 641 students at the Jefferson School?

PRINCIPAL: There is a bilingual program in the Vineyard Elementary School as well as the Jefferson Elementary School.

DON JACINTO: This is not a bilingual program issue. We demand our rights as citizens of the South Side.

PRINCIPAL: The bilingual program is part of Jefferson but cannot bring Vineyard and Jefferson together.

DON JACINTO: I'm glad you mention that. Did your school board know that the program in the South Side has been there for a long, long time? Everybody pays the tuition and you're going to tell me that in our own territory there has been overcrowding for over seven years? Why? Why? What is the reason behind this? Why do you build and add on everywhere else? When will we have our own school? When will we have a new school?

SUPERINTENDENT: Well, Mechanisburg is in close proximity with an additional more and larger school. We decided that there are educational advantages.

TRANSLATOR: [continues to translate and then adds]: In other words, it is a power issue.

DON JACINTO: The children don't have what they need. We need more schools in the South Side. We had three schools knocked down since 1967—all these schools are torn down and only in the South Side.

SUPERINTENDENT: We have eliminated all over the community, not just in the South Side. We spent millions of dollars in the '70s in Mountain Hill and Brookline. This has been fair and equitable with remodeling and elimination.

DON JACINTO: [visibly frustrated] I have so many things to say, so many things to say!

PARENT: What are the other options?

SUPERINTENDENT: The Nasdaq Report suggested a new elementary school, *but* we discounted that suggestion and proposed additions for Easton Hills, *not* the South Side.

Reporters asked questions during this exchange regarding the decision to disregard the suggestion by the Nasdaq Group, which was paid by the school district to study the building needs of the district.

PARENT: If renovation is already taking place, why are we meeting? It has already been decided, it has already started.

SUPERINTENDENT: We are here at the invitation of the Community Council. There was plenty of opportunity when the decision was flexible.This entails $5 to $6 million.

PARENT: In other words, we're in the same situation where we were promised a lot of stuff . . . pool, night classes for parents. We don't have any of that stuff. We paid to start those classes.

SUPERINTENDENT: You refer to the Community School Program led by Dr. Algarin.

PARENT: But we paid our money and received nothing in return!

PARENT: We're going around the point. How many feel insulted? We have to learn about your decisions in the newspaper. As always, you win and we lose. We look like the fools!

PARENT: We are genetically inferior! [referring to an Anglo parent's comment published in the local newspaper].

PARENT: We don't need that racist rhetoric!

SUPERINTENDENT: I'm as upset as you are! I can't apologize for them . . . an anonymous source. We will protect all of our children.

PARENT: Reject that movement to Mechanicsburg.

PRINCIPAL: We do not feel the same way—accept my apologies.

PARENT: I think that a lot has been fermenting. I took a tour of the school . . . safety hazard. There's a problem of a portable added to Jefferson. I hear what the school board said about money, but my concern is about the human element. We have to suffer. Black kids, Latino kids. A good basic education is needed, yet things are slipping. What we need is kids educated. This whole issue is racist. I don't need anybody apologizing about busing our children here to yonder. We know that the population is growing here. We made some mistakes. We got to get better now. We got to work together to get the job done. Don't bring the bilingual program into it. Meantime, what's happening out there. It's a disgrace!

SUPERINTENDENT: This is a first-class school. We have wonderful teachers, a first-class school.

PARENT: Would YOU send your child there? [It is common knowledge that the superintendent does not send his children to the local school.]

PRINCIPAL: The resources are equal to or better than in other schools. Sure, we are overcrowded, but we have also spent an amount of money for lower class sizes and bilingual teachers who are paid more money.

TEACHER: No, no, no. Bilingual teachers are not paid more money!

PARENT: I moved my family here from densely populated New Jersey . . . it doesn't take a Rhoades Scholar to see that the density of the population is here in the South Side.

SUPERINTENDENT: We're addressing the immediate needs.

PARENT: The density factor is *HERE*. We need them here.

PARENT: We live and work in the South Side. We understand the geography, the population growth. The parents of the Raggea School kids were consulted. *WE WERE NOT* consulted. You know that the high influx has been to the South Side. Families with a low income, moderate income, minority families are attracted here. It is an economic issue. When there are limited resources, you look for affordable housing. The affordable housing is here in the South Side. If you bus our children, you're going to have to do it next year, and the following year, and the next year. Jefferson and Vineyard are our major concern. Okay to expand but not solve the long-term incoming needs of the South Side. Why don't you ever bus the white kids? No offense, but our major point is that the problem won't go away by busing our kids. We have a problem that no amount of busing is going to solve. It is scary to us, busing. Granted my children are not in the bilingual program, but that is not the issue.

SUPERINTENDENT: [Referring to the request by one of the school board members to speak] He's one of my bosses!

SCHOOL BOARD MEMBER: Everything makes sense from the other neighborhood. I used to live and skate here. This area is close to St. Loretto's and St. Theresa's. I lived near Vineyard. I was bused to Jefferson when we could not afford the Catholic schools. We were poor people. I still go to Vineyard and the South Side. There will be no discussion because of density to build a new school. This redistricting is for the moment.

TEACHER: *Jamas, jamas* [never, never]; they will never build a new school for the South Side!

PARENT: We moved here from Puerto Rico. My child attends kindergarten. We are just finding out about the redistricting. We're doing the best we can. One person, one parent was quoted in Mechanicsburg [refers to statement by parent in the suburban school rejecting the arrival of the South Side students].

RETIRED TEACHER TO THE BOARD: I just heard you say redistricting for the moment?

BOARD MEMBER: Yes . . . it depends on our projections.

BILINGUAL COORDINATOR: Is it possible to stop the translations since they are taking so much of our time? Does everyone here understand what is being said in English?

PARENT: We have time. [The simultaneous translation is stopped and the rest of the meeting is conducted in English.]

PARENT: You guys are missing the point. Why don't you expand where the football field is? We can use the hills. Schools can be built on hills. We have the engineering and technology to eliminate this problem. We can expand Jefferson and keep our children in the community. The bilingual program is not the issue, but the program was developed to educate children. You're giving us choices? I heard from my job that this was happening.

PRINCIPAL: Schools can be too big, for example, seven hundred to eight hundred children in one school building. It is better too and safer to handle 500 children.

PARENT: I don't agree!

SUPERINTENDENT: We need a long-term solution. Gladys [he refers to the coordinator of bilingual education] has noted the influx of Hispanics. I understand we are not to discuss the bilingual program. In two years we will be in a better position to predict our future needs.

PARENT: I don't think you have to wait two years. We need a solid, long-term plan for the South Side.

PARENT: If you have already decided, why did you call the parents? This reminds me of Bus #57. There are many issues and problems. That bus lost its brakes. My children were on that bus. We need to avoid any problems!

PARENT: Our children are sent everywhere, everywhere! The South Side children are sacrificed. Yet we have more children. We want to avoid any problems.

PARENT: We have been waiting seven years, and now you are saying another two to three years? I heard that the Stony Garden and Mechanicsburg parents have already met. Today, this is the first day that I am aware of your plans. *WE ARE OPPOSED!* We are going to be involved, we will be looking out!

SUPERINTENDENT: The issue about Bus #57 will be checked tomorrow.

PARENT: Why now? [laughter)]. Why not a year ago when a child was almost killed? Whatever you do don't believe everything you read in the paper!

PARENT: Is this an Anglo solution? Where people talk to these people? You seem to be listening, but do you hear? You listen but you do *not* hear. You need to form a group and maybe something will happen. It is not enough to sound off. We need to speak to the *proper* authorities.

PARENT: Does this principal really think the population will drop? This can't wait two to three years. It needs to start now.

COMMUNITY LEADER: The schools differ quite a bit in this district. When you compare the schools for the South Side kids to the Lehightson School for the wealthy white kids you can see the difference. This school district needs to get the word out and show commitment for all of its children.

BILINGUAL COORDINATOR: There may be differences among the schools but not among the teachers. We have excellent Hispanic bilingual teachers. There is no simple solution, but we certainly do not want to add more children to Jefferson. There must be other solutions. The program for bilingual children services our neighborhood. Our teachers give 100 percent. We know that a neighborhood school is needed.

SUPERINTENDENT: A committee to study the long-term solution for the bilingual program has been organized (refers to the Bilingual Education Committee).

ALUMNUS: I was raised in South Side in the 1960s, and now I live in Pittsburgh. I am amazed that the numbers of children are not being considered. These projections have been studied and restudied. I am in awe. As a child I was bused from my home school, where I had attained a 4.0 grade point average, to Washington High School, where my GPA dropped to 2.0 because it affected my self-esteem. I can't believe that this problem has not been solved. *A SCHOOL, ANOTHER SCHOOL,* is needed in this side of town. The students need the bonding, the school spirit. I can't believe this is still happening!

COMMUNITY LEADER: A new school? The solution is a new school? The school board should consider a new school in the South Side.

SUPERINTENDENT: You're so kind. I thank you for your kindness. We appreciate where you're coming from.

DON JACINTO: They're going to be treated bad. They do not want busing. I propose that the children be split (e.g., 50 percent from Lehightson, 50 percent from Jefferson).

SUPERINTENDENT: We will conclude. You've been gracious. I commend you on your interest. Be sure to keep it alive.

TRANSLATOR: Don't forget that there are other issues such as the suspension of Hispanics! Thank you.

Petitions Presented to the School Board

The bilingual parents in the community organized themselves. House-to-house visits were conducted, flyers were distributed, and a petition requesting a new school for the South Side garnered over seven hundred signatures. The next school board meeting on March 14, 1992 was filled with activity, including students carrying placards calling for an end to discrimination. The agenda included the redistricting plans of the school district. The families continued to be optimistic that their voices would finally be heard.

Latino/a children, parents, and leaders spoke before the board that evening. Latino/a leaders speaking before the board included the head of the Community Council, local university professors, a retired and pioneering bilingual educator, a local lawyer, and others who indicated their support for the bilingual families' petition. The children talked about the importance of their school and the bilingual program to their educational lives. The children's voices filled the room with the emotion and the idealism of youth. The retired schoolteacher spoke about the needs of the South Side community as did the head of the Community Council. I spoke that evening (at the families' request) and asked, "Whose knowledge? Whose school? Whose education?" and called for a communication built on *respeto* and a move away from condescending attitudes toward bilingual families. The lawyer talked about the demographic trends and the very specific findings from the reports conducted by the school district. All of the speakers asked that a new school be planned for the South Side children.

Have you ever attended a school board meeting? If you have, it may help you understand why micromanagement approaches can lead to an ego-oriented governance. This totalitarian style of leadership disregards the needs of children for the political benefits of a few. When the decade-old national report calling for reform (*A Nation at Risk: The Imperative for Educational Reform,* (1983) is viewed within the context of this community, it is clear that issues of inequity continue to be evident. My notes of the March 14 meeting, with a few exceptions, depicted a school board that was completely insensitive to the needs of the bilingual community. One or two of the members of this school board attempted to speak on behalf of bilingual children, but were quickly limited by the oppressive tone of the majority. The politics of the situation far outweighed the needs of the children.

The school superintendent's role reminded me of the sheriff's role portrayed in the Montgomery and Birmingham Civil Rights strife of the 1960s. The superintendent stated at a meeting of the Bilingual Committee that he would initiate a campaign by "land, by air, and by sea" in order to eliminate the bilingual program. His intent was to outmaneuver, outwit, and outdistance what he regarded as the "enemy." At the March 14 meeting, he asked the director of the bilingual program and the high school principal to publicly defend the rationale behind housing the bilingual programs in two centers. This was among the first hints in public of what would transpire in the future. The superintendent's campaign to eliminate his school district's bilingual program included media contacts, community meetings, and mandates that disregarded the recommendations of his own faculty, bilingual experts, bilingual parents, community leaders, and the children of Steel Town. The school board continued to present glowing reviews of the superintendent's performance and repeatedly provided generous salary increases.

Reflections by Families and Leaders

The options for the South Side parents (including home schooling) were explored by bilingual families and local community leaders at a meeting at the local community center two days after the March 14 meeting. They considered how to respond to the busing issue and the feeling that there would be no new building for the children of the South Side. The families decided to embrace a "wait and see" attitude. Their disappointment with the school system was evident in spite of the fact that the leaders continued to show guarded optimism if particular strategies could be pursued.

MR. GUERRA: This is a stepping stone situation. A few people have made a miracle. They have never seen so many Hispanics at a school board meeting. It is a winning situation.

MR. MARTINEZ Promise, promise, and insult. Political talk, legal talk.

They want us to be disgusted. They have just put our tails between our legs. If we don't get up and stand up for our rights, we will continue to be at the bottom of the social ladder. We have to use our social power; they have to feel our electoral power.

DON JACINTO: Be alert. There were one hundred yesterday but only twenty today. We need to think about the children.

MR. MARTINEZ: We represent the South Side. We cannot be that whole minority that lives in the South Side. We cannot make decisions for others. If we're going to keep the children home for one year, we have to do it as a whole community.

MR. GUTIERREZ: Did you read Mr. T.'s report where he was cut off at that meeting? There was a 43 percent increase since 1980. We will be 39 percent of the minority by the year 2000. This is not a case of someone who fell asleep at the switch; they are well aware of the crowding. The school board maintains a double standard. The bilingual program is not responsible for the South Side enrollment. They will be held accountable. We will not rest until there is a new school at the South Side.

MINISTER: I am very proud of the Hispanic community. The people mobilized themselves. This is a new trend. The people are fed up. This is not the first time, only the beginning in these schools. As Don Jacinto said, We must do it because of the children. And we will prevail! [Note that this minister and a second minister left Steel Town one year after this meeting.]

DON JACINTO: "El cansansio de los buenos es el triunfo de los malos" [The fatigue of the good is the victory of the bad].

The Elimination of the Bilingual Program

The South Side Latino/o parents continued to object to the school district's decision to bus their children. They requested portable classrooms and ultimately a new school. However, the district's plan to bus 150 students from Jefferson to Mechanicsburg was approved by the school board in spite of parental and community objections. The statement by a parent at the March school board meeting represented the South Side community's sentiment: "Every time a sacrifice needs to be made, it seems the South Side makes it." The petitions signed by the parents, the speeches, the phone calls, the letters, and the children's voices were all silenced.

Media coverage (see chapter 6) and school district activity continued to portray the community's political struggle with a variety of issues. At this time the target became the school district's award-winning (Office of Bilingual Education and Minority Languages Affairs), twenty-year-old bilingual education program. This soon became known as the "bilingual controversy." The school district appointed a committee to review the bilingual program. The Bilingual Committee's report. entitled "Bilingual Program Recommendations" (appendix A), was supportive of the existing program with minor revisions. The school superintendent, in a document entitled "Superintendent's Response to Bilingual Committee's Report" (appendix B), stated his disagreement with the recommendations made by his own faculty about his own school district's program.

The bilingual education program worked well, according to the school superintendent, but he planned to dismantle it At this time, his philosophy supporting English-only immersion programs became public knowledge. He indicated that he did not agree with the bilingual education curriculum of his own district. In his response (see appendix B), he disagreed with his committee's recommendations. He cited a Baker and DeKanter (1981) article and a study conducted with Asian/Pacific Islanders to support his views. He admitted his lack of knowledge about the field of bilingual education and recommended that the school board consider four options. Ultimately the school board agreed to adopt one of the options offered by the superintendent which stated: "Direct that a program be developed to incorporate the philosophical perspective offered by the superintendent." The school superintendent's perspective exemplifies the conservative agenda that has impacted the field of education—what Cummins (1994) has referred to as the "new enemy within."

In spite of community appeals and expert testimony highlighting research findings revealing optimal bilingual educational models, the Carlisle school mentality prevailed. I have used the term "Carlisle school mentality" repeatedly in this text in remembrance of the Native American children who died at the hands of the militarization and assimilation of this group by the Carlisle school in Pennsylvania. The Latino/a children in Steel Town, in the same manner, were forced to assimilate and devalue their language and culture. The sadness in many hearts for Native American children and for Latino/a children in this comunity can be attributed to the disregard by schools and our nation for the needs of bilingual children and families.

On November 12, 1992, Latino leaders filed a complaint with the federal Office for Civil Rights, charging some members of the school district administration with illegal and discriminatory practices. Public comments by school district administrators referred to the South Side schools as "ghetto schools," Latino families as "migrating birds," and Latino fathers as "sex offenders," which continued to fuel feelings of resentment. The school superintendent had no comment for the press, but in a November 14, 1992 article in a local newspaper, he indicated that he was surprised by the opposition to his proposal to change the bilingual program but felt certain he had substantial community support. He stated, "I'm surprised. I knew it's a very emotional issue, and I know there are very strong advocates for it. I (also) know there are people in our community who don't agree with the program."

The editor of a local paper felt that the complaint to the Office of Civil Rights prompted the superintendent "to change his game to hard ball" (November 22, 1992): "Ignoring the thrust of a report by a district task force and his own minority education coordinator, he [the superintendent] asked the board to put an end to Steel Town's bilingual education program."

Steel Town, the Christmas City, was decorated with lights, garlands, bows, and wreaths and filled with the sights and sounds of the holidays. The colorful lights of the South Side community and the monochromatic lights of the northern, more affluent sectors, continued to exemplify the segregated neighborhoods and the differing perspectives. The larger community initiated its holiday fare, while the bilingual families struggled throughout the Christmas season to be heard and to save the bilingual education program.

The families' willingness to search for a quality education flies in the face of stereotypical notions that Latino/a parents are indifferent to their children's educational success. During the hearings and again at the request of bilingual families, I addressed the school board once again:

> It is with a heavy heart that I say to you . . . you [school board and school superintendent] have been hard of hearing and deaf to our [Latino/a] voices, to the voices of children, to the voices of parents, to the voices of teachers, and to the voices of experts. You have created divisiveness with your desire for an English-immersion program. Our children have seen the shouting, the fighting, the anger, the name calling—from "migrating birds" to "jungle savages." We need to model for our children the compassion, the love, the kindness, the understanding, and the wisdom they deserve. I ask you to listen with your hearts and respect the voices here before you. We have a responsibility to make sure that education reflects compassion and humanity.

The school board remained "hard of hearing and deaf" to the community voices. The children in Steel Town continued to hear references to the *Agueybana* families as "jungle savages," "sex offenders," "migrating birds," and "genetically inferior." Christmas 1992 was saturated with the hostile divisive elements of Steel Town, centering on issues of language, culture, and power.

Families living in the area for many years indicated that the question of how to best educate Latino/a children in Steel Town dates back almost a quarter of a century. Latino families said that they felt betrayed by the school superintendent. The director of the bilingual program, in particular, indicated that the district's attention to the language-minority population had been lacking and that dismantling the bilingual program could only worsen the situation. The total number of students in the program was estimated at 1,200, with 94 percent representing Spanish speakers with yearly increasing enrollments for the South Side schools. The resistance by the school board to build a school for the South Side is historically interesting since in 1969 $1.43 million had been set a side for a new school for the South Side's children. According to local newspaper reporters:

In 1969, the district agreed to sell the Washington Elementary School, located on E. 4th Street, to the Steel Town Steel Corp. District officials talked at the time of using the $1.43 million from the sale toward construction of a new Southside school. That was the deal the court approved. But four years later, when Washington finally closed, there was no new school to welcome its students. Instead, they went to Jefferson, which was renovated and expanded. In 1972, the district sought and received permission to free the sale money and use it on other construction projects, especially construction for its Mountain Hill Elementary School. (Martin & Hall 1992)

Families Praying

Mrs. Arroyo, a local parent, referred to the January 28, 1993 school board meeting as the "final nail in the coffin." For others it seemed as if it was the night the lights went out in Steel Town for 1,200 bilingual children, their teachers, and their families.

At the previous school board meeting in December, parents had organized themselves to comment on the bilingual controversy. They found that thirty minutes had been allocated for public comments and that only nine of the registered speakers were heard. The school board effectively foreclosed the Latino families from the discussion. They also effectively changed the agenda. At this meeting, $260,000 was allocated to implement a computer technology pilot program. The computer program was to be tested in one elementary and one middle school as seed money for a $13 million district-wide initiative. The school board decided to postpone matters impacting the bilingual program until late January. The board also limited the time members could talk on issues, with a vote of 5 to 4.

At the January 28 school board meeting in the high school auditorium, most of the more than fifty speakers came to support the district's bilingual program. Over 650 community members participated in this meeting, with large signs and flags dotting the auditorium. Groups of people congregated outside the school building, and groups whispered and talked among themselves until the meeting began. Among the speakers was a local minister who initiated a prayer of petition {a begging prayer} where the bilingual families actually prayed and begged the school board not to dismantle the bilingual education program.

As the minister took the microphone off the stand, he approached the school board and spoke softly: "Bendito, please listen to the parents. I've seen too many kids suffer and too many kids that don't make it. Let's give the kids a chance."

He motioned to the members of his congregation, who walked slowly and peacefully to the front of the auditorium. They stood and prayed in unison in front of the school board. The board members and the security guards were obviously nervous as the minister and his congregation initiated prayers: "Bless this administration. Let them vote in our favor, in favor of our kids. Let us love one another."

The local priest of the Catholic church also called for a compromise from the board and asked them to listen to the recommendations offered by the school-appointed Bilingual Committee that had studied the program for ten months. When Professor Diaz (one of the "success stories" informants) spoke that evening, not only were the security guards noticeably alert, but opponents of the bilingual program shouted and chanted repeatedly, "Sit down, sit down! Shut up, shut up, shut up!" while some supporters responded with, "Let him speak. Let him speak!"

An article describing the January 30 meeting in a local newspaper describes how the superintendent was reacting at this time:

> (Superintendent) said his opinion stands and if Monday's vote goes his way, he foresees the board adopting a program in May or June and putting it into place by the time students return to school in September. "I'm gonna hit the road running Tuesday morning if the board gives me the go ahead. Monday night, (he) said I want to do it fast but I want to do it correctly, I'm not gonna do it wrong, I'm gonna do it right.

The executive director of the Puerto Rican Education Law Center of Pennsylvania questioned the wisdom of the school superintendent in an article in a local newspaper (Mulligan, January 30, 1993):

> Although (the) Superintendent attempts to cloak his arguments as being part of his response to an "educational question" (i.e., how quickly can we get those Hispanic kids to learn English?), I find it rather difficult to overlook how he has ignored the report put together by his own committee of professionals well versed in the field. The sudden concern over the educational achievement of limited English proficiency students came to the surface when the need for a new school in south Steel Town became an ardent issue. If we reject the students' language, then we reject the students' culture. What message are we sending?

One of the reporters polled the school board members at the January 30 meeting and found that the community effort to convince the board to save the bilingual program was in vain. The majority of the board members would vote (6–3) for the English-only immersion model recommended by the superintendent. One of the board supporters of the program, Mrs. Light, expressed disappointment:

> Twenty years in one direction is now dissolved. I'm sad for the little children that enter school for the first time and can speak no English because they will be lost for a long, long time.

Mrs. Light was visibly shaken by a confrontation with four white males at the January 30 meeting. The men shouted and yelled at her when they realized that she had voted on behalf of the bilingual program.

The school district disseminated its "Opening of School" newsletter to parents in early September 1993 and stated:

> On February 1, 1993, the Board of School Directors approved the replacement of the former Bilingual Education Program with an English Acquisition Program. The goal is for limited English proficient students of all nationalities to achieve fluency in English in the shortest amount of time so they may experience maximum success in school. The program will provide for these students in their home schools whenever possible.
>
> A Center for Language Assessment (CLA) will assess new students and recommend placement at the beginner, intermediate, or advanced levels of English acquisition. Professionals at the school will monitor student progress through each level until students exit the program. Periodic review will enable administrators to determine the effectiveness of the overall English acquisition.

The school district document, entitled "A Ticket for Tomorrow . . . English Acquisition Design Team," dated May 24, 1993 (see appendix C), described the English-only program as having a blatantly subtractive philosophy. Interviews with school personnel indicated a "sink or swim" submersion policy, where children were expected to enter mainstream classrooms with minimal help or support. It was not clear how language-minority children would be assessed to determine their "new" placements nor how the ongoing and formative needs would be assessed. The loosely configured statement, "professionals at the school will monitor," appeared to be the school district's assessment strategy. According to Virginia Collier (1992), initial effects of immersion programs can be encouraging due to possible "Hawthorne effects," while the long-lasting effects clearly indicate detrimental outcomes.

In September 1993 a small group of parents whose twenty-three children attended the dismantled bilingual program related their experiences at the beginning of the school year.

MRS. ORTIZ: My son does not want to go to school. The new rules say that you can not speak Spanish in school. They are teaching the children English-only, but there is no content. "My chair is green" is not going to give him knowledge about maps.

MR. RAMIREZ: Since the teacher speaks English only, my wife has to help Carlitos to translate everything into English, then into Spanish, and then back to English. Homework time is tragedy time at my house.

MRS. RIVERA: These [monolingual] teachers talk too fast [to the children] or they talk too slow. . . . They don't understand what they are supposed to do.

MR. GUTIERREZ: The school is violating the civil rights of the bilingual children. After twenty years they should have phased in a new program, no todo de cantaso [not all at once].

MRS. FIGUEROA: No other program in the history of the district has been dismantled for the Anglo parents. Only this program because it affects the Latinos. The teachers were not prepared and there is no program in place.

MRS. ORTIZ: The parents are afraid to speak up.

MR. GUTIERREZ: The American [monolingual] parents have more support. The bilinguals . . . we don't do it porque salimos perjudicados [because it is not to our advantage]. I went to school regarding a bus driver. They call the police on the bilinguals and everyone is afraid. . . . The whites have all the power. The Latinos get into trouble. I've been here twenty years. I went to school here.

MR. RAMIREZ: We don't know what our rights are. Even if we know, we're afraid.

MRS. SANCHEZ: I know I have a right to speak Spanish. I receive respect because I give respect . . . even if they take away my food coupons. I know that there is freedom of speech.

MRS. RIVERA: Some parents have been convinced to believe in this English-only system. I lived it. I know what the problems are.

MRS. FIGUEROA: At Easton Hills, a boy who came here from Puerto Rico took the wrong bus . . . he was hysterical They remembered that I spoke Spanish. We tried to put him on the right bus, but his mother did not have a telephone.

MRS. RIVERA: [summarizing the sentiments of the parents]: We have to learn our rights. El problema Hispano es miedo. We do not have the courage to struggle for what we never had. (The problem for Hispanics is fear).

The *Agueybana* families expressed their despair as they struggled to attain a quality education for their children. Their future vision appeared to dim as their voices continued to be disregarded and the fear (*miedo*), Mrs. Rivera observed, crept into many hearts. How did the media portray the community climate and the events leading to the bilingual controversy? The next chapter documents how political battles were partially fought through the media and how bilingual families continued to struggle for the educational needs of their children.

6

Media Accounts

The "Blue E"

Listeners heard about the "Blue E" on the local radio station. The "Blue E" referred to a proposed city ordinance encouraging local merchants to post a "Blue E" on their doorways to signify their support for the English-only ordinance. The ordinance provided store owners with the ability to price goods based upon the English language proficiency of their prospective buyer. For example, if the store clerk detected an accent or felt that the buyer's English was not up to par, they were expected to pay an additional 10 percent to 20 percent on their purchase since this signified additional paperwork and expense for the merchant.

Supporters of this ordinance called the radio talk show, expressing views such as: "Send all the spics back to their country"; "This is America . . . for whites only"; "Our city was better off without all this trash"; "English is the language my grandparents had to learn"; "One state should be set aside for these people . . . but not Pennsylvania." Only one caller opposed the city ordinance and felt that diverse languages would enhance the tourism industry and the economic well-being of the city. Many of the callers communicated in non-standard American English varieties and dialects. The xenophobic and racist fears described by Crawford (1992) were expressed by most of the callers to the "Blue E" radio talk show.

The manager of the local radio station assured the community that comments and discussions centering on the "Blue E" were a media hoax. "The community need not be alarmed by that discussion," he stated. "Besides, Mr. Jones no longer works for the station and is currently residing in New Jersey." It could be argued that one isolated incident would not be responsible for creating a climate of distrust. Yet to piece many similar incidents together is to gain insights into the many faces of racism and the cumulative effects of oppression in this community. Ultimately, for example, the companion city of Post Town passed an English-only city ordinance while in Steel Town the bilingual program became the center of controversy.

I analyzed the local newspaper accounts (from 1992 to 1993) that reported information on Steel Town's bilingual controversy. These accounts helped uncover how the particular players brought their own meanings to the community context. In many ways the political battles were partially fought through the media as the different players rallied support for their position. Three sets of players represented three major perspectives: English-only proponents, bilingual proponents, and neutral parties. Included in this analysis is a public meeting with over 650 participants.

English-only proponents were comprised of the school superintendent, school board decision makers, and third-generation immigrant citizens who called for the dismantling of the bilingual program. *Bilingual education proponents* were comprised of school personnel, community organizations, community leaders (including clergy), national/local experts, and bilingual families struggling to maintain the bilingual program; and *Neutral parties* were comprised of editors, Raggae School parents, institutions of higher learning, common citizens, and a mediation-type organization that sought to maintain an impartial position.

A timeline of the events will guide the reader in understanding how the circumstances evolved in the Steel Town school district.

Account of Events

March 1992
(a) the school board initiates a one-way busing system of 150 mostly Latino/a children from their South Side home school to a second school and ultimately to a third school

(b) a petition drive is initiated by bilingual families requesting a school for the South Side children and voicing concerns about the education of Latino/a children

November 1992
(c) school-appointed committee report entitled "Bilingual Program Recommendations" (see appendix A) supporting the existing bilingual program is released

(d) public attacks on the bilingual program are initiated by the school district superintendent, including the document entitled "Superintendent's Response to Bilingual Committee's Report," (see appendix B) and some school board members

(e) Steel Town's Action Committee petitions the Office of Civil Rights

(f) the school board decides to delay discussions about the bilingual program until after the holidays

(g) opinions are disseminated in the media indicating support for the bilingual program from experts, educators, families, and children; and support for the school superintendent from school board and selected individuals

(h) the space allocation needs of the school district are discussed as a part of the bilingual program's viability

January, 1993
(i) the school board holds an open meeting on the bilingual program with over 650 community participants and security guards

February, 1993
(j) the school board votes to dismantle the bilingual program
(k) the school initiates an English-immersion planning committee

June, 1993
(l) the report of the school district's English-immersion program entitled "A Ticket for Tomorrow" (see appendix C) is revealed

November 1993
(m) the school board votes unanimously to demolish and rebuild the Raggae School located on the West Side of Steel Town (not the South Side).

The district's choice of construction projects can be seen as a part of the historical context. In 1969, for example, the district agreed to sell a South Side elementary school to a local corporation. The district talked about using the $1.43 million proceeds from the sale for construction of a new school for the South Side, which was approved by the court. Years later there was no new school. Instead, the district sought and received permission from the courts to use the money for other construction projects.

Mr. Berrios, a Puerto Rican doctoral candidate at a local institution of higher learning, summarized his perceptions of the educational controversies:

> When I lived in Puerto Rico, a friend told me about the marvelous schools and educational system the United States has. Moreover, the richness in ethnicity and bilingualism was presented as an integrated fact within the school system. After living in Steel Town for six years and participating as a father of a school-age kid, I regret to say that my friend was wrong; nothing of what he stated happens in Steel Town. Maybe this is personal, but my school district sleeps. In Steel Town the current crisis in education has been defined by color and tone. The words "diversity" and "bilingual" have been used (as) an appropriate tool to politically and aggressively alienate a community that is culturally different. The school district has decided to step backwards and ignore that language, born of culture and ethnicity, which gives voice to the hearts and minds of the individuals who speak it. The educational crisis is characterized by the common causes of power in politics and a clear defiant challenge toward the citizens that do not have access to play the political game as they do.

The "political game" Mr. Berrios described was initiated by the school district superintendent and school board members, who mandated and implemented unilateral decisions impacting the education of bilingual children. Superintendent/board decisions (busing, space allocation, resource allocations, dismantling of the program) led to the political struggle that permeated and divided the community. Bilingual families continued to express frustrations about the quality of education their children were receiving.

The historically "silent ones," the bilingual families of Steel Town, entered the political arena. They first protested decisions to bus their children, requested an additional school in the South Side to alleviate crowding, and opposed the dismantling of a twenty-year-old, award-winning bilingual program. The families' struggle for a quality education included: initiating petition drives; expressing concerns at school board meetings; holding meetings with local and state citizens; contacting local, state, and national experts in the bilingual education field; filing a complaint with the Office of Civil Rights; and running for political office. The major concern expressed by families and community leaders was the educational welfare of bilingual (Latino/a) children.

The March 1992 petition drive against one-way busing garnered over seven hundred signatures with a call for "no more silence" ("se terminó el silencio"). The families asked that a neighborhood school be built for the children of the South Side. They expressed concern about busing young children, overcrowding, and continuing demographic evidence showing increasing numbers of culturally and linguistically diverse children. They indicated that they were willing to temporarily compromise their request if portable classrooms were placed at one of the local schools. The school board, nevertheless, voted to bus the children from their home school to a second school in the fall and ultimately to a third school in the spring. Don Jacinto expressed his sentiments about the school district's continued disregard for bilingual/Puerto Rican children: "build additions to Stony Garden, tear down and rebuild the Raggae School, but can't build a school on the South Side. Why? Because that would be for Puerto Ricans."

The school district appointed a committee comprised of monolingual and bilingual teachers, school administrators, and community leaders to examine the efficacy of the bilingual program. The committee's thirty-four-page report (see appendix A) indicated that, with some modifications, the bilingual program should be maintained. The school superintendent and members of the school board, however, publicly attacked their own program. An article in the local paper (Martin, November 10, 1992) reports the events:

> One thing is clear: Change is coming to the bilingual program in the Steel Town school. But what kind of change—and how it will impact the program's nearly 1,200 students—only grew cloudier after last night's Steel Town Area School Board meeting. Ten months after it began assessing bilingual education, a committee last night recommended some changes but generally urged the board to keep the current model that groups Spanish-speaking students at a few sites and gradually assimilates them into the regular education program by high school.
>
> But the committee's 34-page report drew an immediate challenge and criticism from an unlikely source: the school superintendent. "I have had and continue to have a deep concern about the length of time we keep children in this program

and out of regular education," he said. "I do not see a need to maintain any one particular ethnic group's culture via the school system."

He heard no dispute from the board.

In a possible sign of the future, the directors almost uniformly expressed concerns about the program and recommendations. "I think we need to make a concerted effort to get the students out of the program as soon as possible," said director Johnson. About 94% of this year's bilingual program students speak Spanish; the remaining students speak a total of 18 other languages.

The board vice president called the current model "overkill." The school superintendent said he has his own recommendation for the bilingual program, but that he will present them to the board at another time.

Another newspaper article (Schnur, November 10, 1992) also documented the superintendent's and the school board's public comments at this time. The headline read, "School superintendent criticizes bilingual program," and continued:

The Steel Town superintendent told the school board Monday the district's bilingual program doesn't move students into regular English-only classes quickly enough, despite findings in a report that mostly supports the current system. 'We've got to throw them into the pool. They'll swim,' the school superintendent said. 'With a little help from us they'll swim."

On Monday, the board was presented with a report from a committee of community members, teachers, and administrators that supports the current system with some modifications. . . . But the school superintendent disagreed with the report. The superintendent advocates a system where students go directly into classes taught in English by bilingual teachers who can translate something into Spanish if a student is confused . . . while the board vice president indicated that "he agreed with the school superintendent '100 percent.'"

A local Spanish-speaking newsletter found humor in the superintendent's remarks. disseminating a cartoon depicting the superintendent literally "throwing" children off a dock and into a lake. His statements became a "red herring," a clear signal to the bilingual program proponents about his intent. His perspective was translated as supportive of a "sink or swim" philosophy outlawed by legal statutes, including the U.S. Supreme Court (*Lau v. Nichols*, 1974). I found it intriguing that the school superintendent's ethnic origin is Portuguese. It was not possible to obtain information about how he feels about his own ethnicity, language knowledge, and his family's immigration process. My repeated requests for meetings with the superintendent were denied. I suspected that he clearly understood my opposition to his philosophy and was reluctant to discuss issues dealing with bilingualism.

The bilingual controversy was burning brightly with supporters and opponents. Graduate students in a summer course I taught examined the controversy. The students collected and critiqued the ongoing media discussions. We invited and informally interviewed reporters, community representatives, and school district leaders well versed on the bilingual controversy.

I have not shared those interviews here since complete confidentiality was assured all of our invited guests. My students continued their own fact finding, however, and reported many more community groups and individuals who supported the bilingual program than opposed it. My students indicated that the opponents— the local superintendent, school board members, and several individuals—were ultimately the privileged power brokers.

Newspaper reporters who tried to make sense of the controversy included the following:

> Both sides in the debate over the future of bilingual education in city schools say they have the best interest of the children at heart. The superintendent and some members of the school board say the Latino students need to learn English faster. The Latino community, bilingual teachers, and school administrators say the current program is working just fine. (Schnur, November 14, 1992)

After the Bilingual Committee's report, the school superintendent announced the four options he planned to offer the school board: (1) accept the recommendations of the Bilingual Committee; (2) accept the school superintendent's philosophy and develop a new bilingual program; (3) develop a pilot program to test how effectively the school superintendent's ideas work; or (4) hire an objective consultant to evaluate the district's program.

The school superintendent indicated to the press that he was "surprised" at the Latinos' response, but that he had a great deal of support for his position.

> "I'm surprised. I knew it's a very emotional issue, and I know there are very strong advocates for it," said the school superintendent. "I know there are people in our community who don't agree with the program."
>
> The school superintendent said he has turned the prospect of a civil rights complaint over to the district's solicitor, who was unavailable for comment yesterday. (Hall, November 14, 1992)

> At the next school board meeting, the school superintendent described his program plans, indicating that he proposed an intensive program that would have children learning English in a year, if possible. He could not say how that would be done. "I'm not an expert," he said. "That's for people to design."
>
> In other business, the school superintendent received a 5.5 percent raise with a one percent merit bonus, raising his salary to $95,024. (Schnur, November 17, 1992)

The following day the school superintendent confessed his (lack of) expertise in the field of bilingual education: "I'm not an expert on bilingual education," he said. "I just know that we need to shorten the time line of the program" (Snyder, November 18, 1992).

In subsequent newspaper articles the week of November 20, monolinguals' community support for the superintendent's position appeared with the typical "when my grandparents came to this country" argument, reflecting third-generation immigrant perspectives:

> When my grandparents came to this country from their native land, they did not speak English. They did not expect anyone to cater to them and change everything into their native tongue. In fact, they did not even teach their children their native language; they believed their children were Americans and so should speak the language of America. Perhaps it is time for people who intend to make America their homeland to adopt this philosophy also. (Comment, November 20, 1992)

A local school principal interviewed by reporters indicated his perspective:

> The district has no statistics comparing the Latino bilingual program and the non-Latino program. "Stony Garden Elementary School didn't have a teacher to give English lessons to its German and Arab students until early this month," the school principal said. The school principal thinks Latino students should take classes in English (only) rather than Spanish. "I'm supportive of what the superintendent is saying," said the school principal, a Greek-American. He said he learned English more quickly by being immersed in the language. "We got by," he said. (Schnur, November 21, 1992)

An outsider and invited guest at a local college was also willing to speak to the issue by attempting to draw comparisons among ethnically diverse populations:

> William Andersen isn't sure how well bilingual education is working. (The) Director of (a) national office spoke about bilingual education facing the Steel Town Area School District. "The Asian community has found ways to succeed through cultural barriers by simply working harder at it. . . . I think we must find a way to create a support system to encourage the same results for the Hispanic and African American communities." (Williams, January 24, 1993)

Supporters of the bilingual program and the Bilingual Committee's report included community organizations, bilingual families, community leaders, and experts in the field of bilingual education. The Community Council, a grassroots organization, was concerned with educational issues impacting language-minority speakers. The president of the council supported the committee's report:

These are recommendations that were thoughtfully, thoroughly discussed by teachers who instruct these students and many of whom have had special training in educating second language students. We believe their recommendations are sound and worth listening to. (Schnur, November 13, 1992)

The organization denounced the superintendent for his "negative comments regarding the bilingual education program and his belief that the use of Spanish as a language of instruction is un-American." The superintendent was also criticized for his support of an "immersion" approach that expected students who speak little or no English to be taught in English, thinking they would learn the language faster.

The school superintendent objects to the teaching of the culture of Hispanic students even when they comprise 21.4 percent of our school population, and indications are that this number will increase. (Kupper, November 13, 1992)

Steel Town's Action Committee, an advocacy group, indicated that they were prepared to file a federal civil rights complaint if the district changed the bilingual program. They stated:

Our organization takes exception with his [superintendent's] comments that our schools need not teach Latino culture. Since by the superintendent's own admission the bilingual education program works, well, then the Steel Town Action Committee is prepared to insure that the civil rights of our Latino youth are not violated by eliminating a portion of a program solely based on the biases toward a particular ethnic group, in this case Latino children. (Hall, November 14, 1992)

The complaint to the Office of Civil Rights became a reality:

Latino leaders living in the Steel Town Area School district have filed a complaint with the federal Office for Civil Rights, charging some members of the district administration with illegal and discriminatory practices. "It is our belief that the district through the actions of some of the members of the present administration have engaged in acts that are morally indefensible and clearly illegal. . . . This is indicative of the view that somehow schools on the Southside and students who go to them are less than anyone else.

The Action Committee is asking the Philadelphia OCR to conduct an independent investigation. The complaint was filed Thursday. The committee was represented by (an) attorney of Steel Town. The Committee cited the U.S. Constitution, the Equal Opportunity Education Act of 1974, the 1964 Civil Rights Act, Title VI, the Lau v. Nichols case guidelines, and federal case law as standards to measure the district's alleged shortcomings. (Politi, November 16, 1992).

The issues cited in the OCR complaint included unequal treatment of students, harassment, disproportionate suspensions, the "proposed dismantling of the bilingual program linked to the school superintendent's personal bias against primary language instruction and to not wanting to provide equitable space in the Southside schools which are operating at near functional capacities," and mistreatment of the 1,200 bilingual students (94% Latino/a).

The night the committee's report was presented, the bilingual coordinator stated:

> A lot of nurturing takes place. . . . The committee really believes this is the best program. . . . Studies show children need five to seven years before they speak a new language well enough to do well in academic classes in that language. (Schnur, November 14, 1992)

Bilingual experts also came to the defense of the bilingual children and families:

> James Lyons, a national proponent for bilingual education also slammed the school superintendent's proposal yesterday. "I don't know of a single educational authority that has said it's even a plausible goal for a child in a year," said Lyons, the executive director of the National Association for Bilingual Education. "A year is just poppycock." He said the district should continue with bilingual education classes. "Students who receive instruction in their native language learn English better, and they do not lose valuable time in other subjects, such as math and science, " he said.
>
> "In the school district of Annville, students in bilingual classes drop out of school less than students in any other program in the district," said the Annville district program coordinator. "The dropout rate is about 5 percent in the bilingual program," he said. "Students who participate in the bilingual program perform equal to or better than other students on standardized tests," Lyons said. "It's certainly proven itself in this district." (Snyder, November 18, 1992)

At the time, I was an associate professor of education at a local university and indicated to the press that much research supports having classes taught in the native language:

> The very best way to teach children English is to make sure their home language and home culture is intact. Dr. Soto called the school superintendent's proposal "educationally unsound." (Snyder, November 18, 1992)

The children and families spoke on their own behalf at meetings and in the media. Bilingual students and families appeared in newspaper stories and in photo essays, for example:

> Latino students begged the school board not to change the district's bilingual program. Some students carried signs saying things like, "Inequity=academic failure=high drop out rates." (Schnur, November 17, 1992)

> Education shows love, Latino father says. Chevere's two sons are among he 1,200

non-English-speaking students enrolled in the Steel Town District's bilingual education program, 94 percent of them Latino. (Hall, November 22, 1992)

High school students' voices were heard at school board meetings and from local reporters. Maria Rivera organized groups of students, who carried banners at meetings, spoke at the school board's "courtesy of the floor," and were represented in the media accounts:

> The superintendent's plan of "English immersion" shouldn't be tried, according to several students. When Maria Rivera arrived in Steel Town from Puerto Rico 16 months ago, she knew very little English and very little about politics. Maria, a junior at Steel Town High School, speaks English clearly now and sometimes she speaks it fiercely, defending a program that she believes is helping her and her younger sisters and brother succeed in the United States. She and several of her classmates in the high school's English as a Second Language program have been fighting the school superintendent in his bid to change the bilingual education program.
>
> Felipe Rodriquez is a Steel Town junior, who came to Steel Town from Puerto Rico 2 1/2 years ago. He says that without a program like the one he's experienced, "I would be completely lost. . . . It's like you have lions in a cage and you put in a little goat," he says. "It's so hard to come out of that cage and break out." (Mulligan, January 28, 1993)

The nearby twin city of Post Town passed an English-only ordinance in 1994, but its Latino leaders showed support for families struggling with the bilingual controversy in Steel Town.

> Bilingual education is a community wide issue, Dr. Rodriguez said. He feels the Hispanic community, which already has a high dropout rate among students, will suffer even more if the bilingual program is removed. (Williams, January 23, 1993)

Where were the neutral parties and possible mediators throughout the bilingual controversy? One community organization comprised of mostly Anglo citizens held a series of meetings in an attempt to act as mediators. Basic information about the field was shared in an informal manner. When I presented information to this group, one of the members accused me and the bilingual families of Steel Town of having a "hidden agenda." It was not clear to me what they meant by these attacks. The only hidden agenda I understood was an agenda that would provide access to quality programs for children. Unfortunately these efforts were only helpful to the English-only proponents. Individuals in the group with noble intentions were silenced by more fearful and suspicious elements.

It probably makes more sense to group the neutral parties with the English-only advocates because historically a neutral philosophy can ultimately lead to tragic losses. Those of us who grew up as baby boomers can relate many national and international examples that have ultimately resulted in the loss of life, including the Civil Rights Movement, the Holocaust, Native American genocide, and recent ethnic cleansing in Bosnia.

In this study, various dynamics were observed among the neutral persons. For example, local university administrators who appeared to support the bilingual proponents at the onset of the bilingual controversy declared their neutrality after receiving telephone calls from the local superintendent. It was difficult for me to understand the rationale and thinking of my colleagues and my own educational leader, who confessed to me in whispered tones, "You know, I just don't want to be seen as supporting the Latinos." What does that mean? Does danger lurk somewhere for those who support "the Latinos"? How much courage does it take for an educator to stand up on behalf of equity? Are the conservative opinions of a superintendent czar more important than children's well-being? Whatever happened to freedom of speech?

There were two additional sources in the media that could also be portrayed as neutral mediators but whose well-intentioned efforts were also not helpful to the bilingual families and children struggling to have their voices heard. First, a columnist, and then an editor of a local newspaper:

> Bilingual education debaters both want what's best.
> Neighborhood Column:
> Nobody is using the "c" word, but it's just below the surface of conversation in Steel Town these days. Coddle. The Bilingual Coordinator says the bilingual program is taking the rap for the failure of Latino students who were never enrolled in it. "The public is being led to believe the program is the failure," the Bilingual Coordinator says. "These (bilingual students) are the ones who are actually faring better."
> But the school board has difficult questions to ask itself before making a decision. For example, if the bilingual program doesn't work, why does the Latino community want to keep it? Latinos have been vocal and organized about other issues like a police substation for Southside and improvements for Jefferson Elementary School. If the bilingual program was failing them and preventing them from getting better jobs, wouldn't they be the first ones to demand change? (November 19, 1992)

> *Editorial*
> The debate over bilingual education does not have to tear Steel Town apart. It is true that decisions about how to teach children for whom English is a second language carry with them a great deal of emotional baggage. And, they get tangled with other complicated issues, such as overcrowding and the fairness with which the Steel Town Area School District allocates its resources. But the best hope to resolve

this matter—and to make the schools better for everyone—is to be careful about defining the issues. We must start not with the bilingual program itself, but with the widespread belief in the Latino community that the school district puts its children second. The uneven application of discipline, a lack of new texts for Hispanic students and overcrowding of schools that serve neighborhoods where Hispanics predominate are only part of their grievances. There is also the perception that some principals and other Steel Town administrators are prejudiced against non-white and Hispanic students. A task force on school space acknowledged that one way to reduce crowding at Jefferson and Vineyard schools is to end the bilingual programs, which bus children from around the district to those buildings. It will be the school district's shame if, in effect, it tells Latinos, you can have a bilingual program or you can have less-crowded schools, but you can't have both. (November 22, 1992)

The debate continued in the community with the school board announcing that it wanted to resolve the bilingual program question by January. Two of the school board members voiced opinions unlike their counterparts: "It's more than just a bilingual curriculum issue," said a school board member. "This is an ethnic issue. This is, in some people's mind, a race issue." A second board member indicated: "I sense a distrust of our schools in relation to Latino children" (Martin, November 30, 1992). Three of the school board members would later vote for keeping the bilingual program.

The struggle continued as two possible dates for the public informational meeting regarding the bilingual program were announced by the board. The meeting would be scheduled for either January 12 or January 25, depending on the board's scheduling conflicts. A separate public hearing was scheduled for January 28 (Kopacki, January 5, 1993). The superintendent was quoted as saying, "I want to nail this one and I want the best for our students" (Mulligan, January 12, 1993). The superintendent wrote the following column:

Express Yourself
by the School District Superintendent
Proposal for bilingual education stresses acquiring English early.
I oppose many of the committee's recommendations and have stated my reasons publicly. I have received an overwhelming number of letters and calls from people supporting my position. In a nutshell, the debate hinges on three central issues: The length of the program; maintenance of culture for Latino students in the bilingual program; lack of social integration of Latino students into the English-speaking student population. On Nov. 16, I recommended to the school board an outline for a new program. Its main premise is early English acquisition, which would ensure success equipping students with the ability to communicate in the language of this country—English! The fact is that English immersion programs are legal and have been implemented successfully all over the United States for many years. The question of building a new elementary school on the Southside has nothing to do with

bilingual education. As superintendent, please know that my single motivation for changing the current bilingual education program is my deep and sincere belief that the earlier children master the English language, the better their chances for success. (January 27, 1993)

This opinion piece was published just prior to the public hearing and reflects issues of power and the conservative agenda sweeping institutions of learning. Aronowitz and Giroux (1985) have described the conservative vision in a book entitled *Education Under Siege,* while Cummins (1994) refers to the "new enemy within." The superintendent's letter reflects this agenda.

Prior to the public hearing, teachers were asked to provide information about their bilingual students. Some of the teachers indicated that they were "ordered" to rate individual student performance without any instructions as to the purpose of the data gathering. "We were told that either the teachers do the evaluations or they would be done by an administrator," a middle school teacher said. A Jefferson teacher commented, "I assumed it was to place the kids, group them for next year." The teachers felt left out of the whole decision-making process about the bilingual education program. "Quite honestly, I don't think that any of us know what's going down," said a middle school teacher (Martin, January 28, 1993).

The January public hearing reflected anticipation, excitement, and preparation on the part of the speakers. Amid the cheers, boos, and flag waving, a nine year old silenced the crowd. The board seated at the front of the high school auditorium became noticeably frightened when a congregation knelt and prayed on behalf of the bilingual children in Steel Town. The board's fear of the bilingual participants was unwarranted, but board members supportive of the bilingual program were confronted at a subsequent meeting by white males who shouted and gestured," You people don't understand what's happening." They called the board members "incompetent" and added that "white middle class people end up bearing the cost of education for Spanish-speaking students." (Mulligan, February 2, 1993)

Martin (1993), in one of the newspaper accounts, noted that at this meeting the decision to dismantle the bilingual program had already taken place. The bilingual proponents had been silenced, even before they spoke at this meeting. This was Martin's account of the public hearing:

Steel Town High Crowd Urges Keeping Bilingual Program—
Board Supports Immersion
With flags, signs, emotion, and concern, about 650 people crowded Steel Town High School auditorium last night to deliver messages to the Steel Town Area School Board. "If you take away the bilingual program in Steel Town, you take away the Latino students' chances of learning," said a high school student, "and gradually

they will become frustrated and drop out." For three hours the crowd hooted and howled, clapped and cheered. Pastors sermonized. Students testified. Others criticized in English and Español. But all may have been for naught. Four of the nine board members polled after the meeting said they would vote Monday to replace the current program.

Said a teacher, "If we reject the student's language, we also reject the student's culture. What message are we sending?" A nine year old silenced the crowd with his soft, innocent voice. "When I started here, I did not know English," said the nine year old, an Argentinean who attended the bilingual program at Vineyard. "I also learned lots of English," he said, "As you can now tell."

Toward the end a pastor called the crowd to the front of the auditorium. More than 100 people marched to the table of board members. Some handed the school superintendent a folder crammed with petitions signed by parents of students in the bilingual program. The pastor prayed. "Bless these administrators," he said, eyes closed. "Let them vote in our favor, in the favor of our kids." The vice president of the board said later he appreciated the blessing, but that he had seen the light before the hearing. "I've heard them all before," he said. (Martin, January 29, 1993)

The roles of the local pastor and a local priest were captured by Mulligan in the January 29, 1993 article:

The pastor of the Church on Steel Town's Southside took the microphone off its stand and approached board members, speaking softly, "Bendito, please listen to the parents," he said. "I've seen too many kids suffer and too many kids don't make it. Let's give the kids a chance." Facing the audience, the pastor motioned Latino members to come to the front and began to pray as board members found themselves looking up at a solid wall of standing people. "Bless this administration. Let us love."

The two security guards tensed.

The priest of (the) Church called for a compromise, asking that the school board extend its Monday deadline and heed the recommendations of the committee that studied the program for 10 months to keep it intact and consider revisions. "It seems to me unfair to truncate their work," he said.

As the school board continued to discuss the decision regarding the bilingual program, some members of the board revealed their doubts while others requested additional information. The final 6 to 3 vote was cast in February, supporting the school superintendent's proposal calling for English by immersion for children who spoke little or no English to "become fluent in English in the shortest amount of time so they may experience maximum success in school" (Mulligan, February 2, 1993). The three school board members who dissented expressed their disappointment and faced confrontations with English-only proponents.

The high school students who had been so active in their support of the bilingual program were described by one of their teachers as feeling "depressed because they put a lot of time into it. They did a great job. They did all that they possibly could and there were things that they said and did that definitely had a positive effect in the community" (Mulligan, February 3, 1993). Maria Rivera, the student who organized her peers, continued to express optimism.

The English Acquisition Design Team appointed was comprised by a new set of players (largely monolingual and monocultural this time) and led by the school administration to begin its design of an English-immersion program. A consultant from a nearby state was asked to speak at an all-day meeting with the newly formed committee. The committee's report, presented in June, was entitled "A Ticket for Tomorrow" (see appendix C). The program included a buddy system, pairing language-minority students with English speakers. At least one of the school board members (Mrs. Light) expressed concern about the programmatic implications of the report:

> I'm very concerned about the elementary school proposal. According to the report, most elementary school students who would have been placed in the bilingual programs . . . will now be placed in regular all-English classes in their home schools and receive 75 minutes a day of English for speakers of other languages instruction. They'll be frustrated when classes are totally in English. (Mulligan, June 14, 1993)

The design team released its report as the English-immersion plan for the school district. The plan outlined relates a program design acquired during a visit to a school district in a nearby state that had been previously successful in a court battle involving issues of English as a second language. A retired school district principal, who referred to Latino families as those "migrating birds" and Latino fathers as "sex offenders," was instrumental in initiating this contact. The fact that this district was successful in court prompted the district administration to reason that they, too, could stand up to the local leaders' existing Office of Civil Rights complaint.

The Steel Town school district continued to make decisions that disregarded the needs of the South Side bilingual families while at the same time they rewarded the West Side largely monolingual families. Initially during the controversy, bilingual families collaboratively reached out to the Raggae Parent and Teacher Association (PTA), who seemed supportive. One of the PTA leaders met me in a parking lot near my office, whispering that they could no longer support the bilingual families. Apparently the school superintendent met with parents of the Raggae School, offering to assist with a new building for their children. The message the monolingual parents received was that silence could prove valuable. In November 1993 the outcome was evident:

> The school board voted unanimously to raze the 75-year-old (Westside) Raggae Elementary School once another the same size is built behind it. The $3.4 million

project won't begin for about a year, but the money is already guaranteed through a bond issue the board approved last summer. The state will reimburse the district for $620,300 of the cost.

Also last night, the board decided by a 7–1 vote to give the school superintendent a raise from his annual salary of $94,732 to $98,152. The vote came after a glowing evaluation of the school superintendent's service was read into the record.

Before the Raggae vote, the president of Parents and Teachers of Raggae School joined a parent in asking that the new building remain a neighborhood school of about 300 students. (Bronstein, November 16, 1993)

Whose education and whose schooling is reflected in Steel Town? Power became an important element during Steel Town's bilingual controversy. Issues of power continued to be evident in November 1993, when the school board voted to demolish and rebuild the Raggae School in a non-South Side neighborhood. The call for a neighborhood school for 300 students at Raggae begs the question: What about the 1,200 children represented by the bilingual education proponents? Why were 1,200 children's educational needs sacrificed in this political struggle? Will language-minority children in Steel Town live long enough to experience educational equity? What is the role of the Office of Civil Rights with regard to language-minority children in Steel Town?

One of the bilingual program supporters was so moved by the events that he wrote the following poem:

Under the Cover of Darkness
by Sis-Obed Torres Cordero
December 18, 1992

Under the Cover of Darkness driven men hitched horses
in preparation for rides pre-planned under the burning sun.
Targets were selected to use "as examples" or for retaliation for slights,
real or imagined.
Coordinated psychological terror.
When will they visit again? Today? Tomorrow?
Wood-shaped symbols of Eternal Salvation, ablaze, seared into the national
subconscious sending primal fears, goose bumps down, from the nape of
the neck to the small of the back.
Be quiet. Silence or death, night or day, open your mouth,
you are "free" to choose, but "remember your place."
Stillness imposed.
People were watched during the day while whispers fanned the winds.
We are going to get you, quietly, effectively,
creating doubt in the minds of others,
don't speak out.
The undercover Riders lived among neighbors, friends,
family who knew it was criminal,

UN-Holy, morally indefensible, unjust,
but the Riders quietly observed and controlled the watch.
Deep down in the hearts of many,
those "who knew" stood transfixed:
mannequin spectators,
the Christians and the lions,
minds encased, empty, shrouded in the knowledge
coffins are made to be filled with tongueless, welded mouths.
To stand up for the natural human rights of other means to
abandon zombie lives and risk shunning, death or excommunication from
the body politic.
The Eternal Order of "Don't Cross That Line"
replaces the Souls of the living.
Yesterday, Today and Tomorrow.
Under the Cover of Darkness,
"The Lynching Rope" is replaced by sophisticated jaws in the Coliseum.
In the name of the majority,
the devouring Lion of Public Opinion is primed to destroy humans in being.
Witness the spectacle.
They will try to discredit you, dishonor you, disrobe you in public, humiliate
you in the eyes of your peers, threaten you with unemployment so that you
will go away.
Death by Public opinion. The New Hanging Rope.
Shame.
Spectators suffer from paralyzed hearts pounding to conserve precious
blood.
Of what use is that blood when we continue to allow those under cover of
darkness
to operate freely?
The only power that defeats fear is the power that comes from the Soul.
Once fear is defeated, to live in silenced submission is no longer a viable
alternative.
It is within your power to choose.
Silence=Death. Choose wisely.

This defeat was personally difficult for children, leaders, and families who were proponents of the bilingual program. Threats, confrontations, and lost jobs resulted from Steel Town's bilingual controversy. The treatening phone calls I received late at night prompted my graduate students and colleagues to offer assistance on the matter, but other players were not as fortunate as I was. Ultimately the political struggle led to a variety of losses to children, families, and the community. Chapter 7 explores these losses and the accompanying advice from families who struggled on behalf of their children, while the epilogue shows how the lives of the participants continue to evolve.

7

Restoring the American Dream

A Light Shines in Steel Town

John F. Kennedy (1962) said, "The greatest enemy of the truth is very often not the lie, deliberate, continued and dishonest—but the myth—present, persuasive, and unrealistic." Has the myth of the American Dream become a nightmare for language-minority children?

Families of color in America have lived the daily realities of a rising neo-conservative agenda in America. Contemporary examples of how bilingual families are being impacted by an oppressive and blatantly racist agenda include the proliferation of the English-only movement, the passage of California's Proposition 187, and legislative budgetary mandates punishing the most vulnerable in our nation. According to Giroux (1995), America is experiencing a popular contruction of a "national identity that is read as white, heterosexual, middle class, and allegedly threatened by contamination from cultural, linguistic, racial, and sexual differences" (48).

> For many Americans, questions of national identity seem to elude the complex legacy of nationalism and take on a mythic quality. Informed by the powerful appeal to assimilation and the legitimating discourse of patriotism, national identity often operates within an ideological register untainted by the historical and emerging legacies of totalitarianism. (45)

The Steel Town community exemplifies how power relations impact the quality of children's educational programs. The political struggle that ensued during the bilingual controversy led to asymmetrical power relations. The ultimate outcome for children was a monolingual, monocultural education. The report from the English Acquisition Design Team entitled "A Ticket for Tomorrow" (see appendix C) documents the school's English-only curricular intent. Freire and Macedo (1987) note that: "The English (only) movement in the United States points to a xenophobic culture that blindly negates the pluralistic nature of U.S. society and falsifies the empirical evidence in support of bilingual education, as has been amply documented" (154).

The bilingual families' struggle on behalf of their children was overshadowed by a Carlisle school mentality. An oppressive agenda by the school leaders dominated

83

the community, resulting in a number of losses, including bilingual educational opportunities for children and a political voice for bilingual families. Steel Town allowed a racist climate to dominate bilingual families and perpetrate what Freire (1970) describes as "cultural invasion": "invaders penetrate the cultural context of another group, in disrespect of the latter's potentialities; they impose their own view of the world upon those they invade and inhibit the creativity of the invaded by curbing their expression" (150).

The data showed bilingual families to be knowledgeable about best educational practices. Families provided advice about bilingual education to the school that is congruent with research evidence. The more powerful, oppressive elements, however, obscured the families' advice and wisdom, allowing children's home languages and cultures to be devalued. Cummins (1994) distinguished between collaborative power and coercive power in his Keynote speech at a NABE Conference. He described exemplary programs that were collaborating with their communities (e.g. Foundation's Center early childhood program).

Elements of power can be viewed as intervening within community contexts that value or devalue home languages and cultures. Coercive power is capable of imposing oppression, abuse, inequity, and totalitarianism, and of violating human rights and freedoms. Collaborative power, on the other hand, affords a community democratic expression, human rights, and freedom. The theoretical framework presented in table 1 shows the outcomes schools can anticipate with the use of coercive or collaborative power. These power models can impact children's educational experiences.

Table 7.1. The Relation of Language, Culture, and Power to Schooling

Community Relations	Intervening	Anticipated Outcomes
Democratic {Value Languages & Cultures}	<Collaborative Power>	English-plus multilingualism bicultural identity languages preserved equal opportunity political voice
Oppressive {Devalue Languages & Cultures}	<Coercive Power>	English-only language domination cultural invasion loss of human rights unequal opportunity silenced voice

The dynamics of the coercive power relations in Steel Town included at least three major elements of oppression: (1) the English-only, xenophobic environment;

(2) Freire's notion of cultural invasion; and (3) language domination. The language domination discouraged and actively prevented families from speaking their home language at school and at home. These oppressive elements systematically silenced children and families, forcing them to struggle with Steel Town's disrespect for their bilingualism and biculturalism.

The community relations existed as a continuum reflecting the strength of an oppressive climate that devalues language and culture versus a democratic climate that values language and culture (see figure 7.1).

Fig. 7.1. Continuum of community relations

+	oppressive climate	democratic climate	+
	devalues languages & cultures	values languages & cultures	

The status of languages and the types of power exerted in this community influenced decisions directly relating to the daily educational realities children experienced in classrooms. The disregard of the Bilingual Committee's report, "The Blue E" (the English-only city ordinance), and the elimination of the bilingual program are examples of coercive political power.

Finally, the strength of the oppressive climate silenced the very voices representing children's bilingual educational opportunities. Steel Town's neo-conservative, xenophobic, oppressive relations silenced bilingual voices, created language domination, promoted cultural invasion, and resulted in disrespect for bilingualism and biculturalism. Just as the Carlisle Native American Indian School practiced genocide, so have contemporary schools continued to perpetrate the educational genocide of bicultural children. In a democratic society

> an individual can be bicultural and still be loyal to American ideals. educational environments or policies that do not recognize the individual's right, as guaranteed by the Civil Rights Act of 1964, to remain identified with the culture and language of his [her] cultural group, are culturally undemocratic. (Ramirez & Castaneda 1974, 23)

Valuing Language and Culture

Ensuring that children with limited English proficiency are not handicapped in their schooling is the goal of bilingual education. According to the U.S. Commission on Civil Rights (1975), "Lack of English proficiency is the major reason for language minority students' academic failure. Bilingual education is intended to ensure that students do not fall behind in subject matter content while they are learning English, as they would likely do in an all-English program." In addition, children who do not

speak the school language are "effectively foreclosed from any meaningful education," according to the U.S. Supreme Court (*Lau v. Nichols,* 1974).

> Experience has shown that where no bilingual program exists, Hispanic parents are
> less likely to approach the school and talk with teachers, that children are neglected
> by their teachers and tend to drop out, and that little effort is made to teach them
> English, preferring instead to classify them as slow learners or retarded. Indeed
> these and other evils provided the impetus for bilingual education in the first place.
> (Otheguy 1991, 419)

Data obtained from the National Clearinghouse for Bilingual Education (1995)
reports an upward trend in the "limited English proficient student population
(LEP)" in the past eight years. The most recent figures available show a 13 percent
increase over the previous school year (1992–93 school year); 9.2 percent was the
average yearly increase of LEP from 1985 to 1993. LEP students are younger (more
than two out of three are in grades K–6), and three out of four LEP use Spanish as
their native home language. In light of the continued educational needs of second-
language speakers, it will be important for schools to pursue collaborative democratic
power models.

Four stages of societal development affecting attitudes and policies toward
bilingual education are described by Lewis (1980). The first stage consists of control
over minority and linguistic groups. The second stage emphasizes cultural assimilation, while the third stage emphasizes the national language but tolerates minority
languages as a means of promoting mass literacy needed for a usable workforce. The
fourth stage, which may be the key to why the superintendent cut the bilingual program, introduces the idea that bilingual education would explicitly be concerned
with the redistribution of political power.

The final stage described here was what the larger Steel Town community
feared. It was evident that even a hint of power redistribution met with massive
resistance as evidenced by the suprintendent's motto to fight families "by air, by
land, and by sea." The persistent silencing of voices may lie in Steel Town's perceived
threats from the language-minority groups. Yet the coercive power tactics can be
likened to destructive chemical warfare on a peace-loving, peacekeeping people.

The oppressive tactics helped obscure the future needs of a community in dire
need of technological, scientific, and industrial advances for a stronger economic
base. The larger community ignored the fact that providing educational opportunity
leads to academic school achievement and cognitive learning. Quality learning can,
in turn lead to multiple "success stories." Data showed how the families with "success stories" were intent on providing services to Steel Town with a cultural attitude
of returning what has been given. The medical doctors interviewed, for example, initiated a free clinic for poor children, the lawyer provided services in kind, and educa-

tors led a variety of community organizations. The caring instruction the families modeled at home was extended to the ecological context of the community as families showed a willingness to reach out to the community well beyond their professional duties.

The *Agueybana* families, the bilingual families, did everything possible at home as they struggled to meet their children's educational needs. The families shed light on a community with an oppressive climate. Their resilience, courage, and persistence within a hostile environment were admirable as was the wisdom they disseminated. Interviews showed bilingual families deliberately fostering family cohesion. A home language caring environment was at the heart of the home instruction.

Parents who majored in education (at their respective universities) relied on the one parent–one language strategy during their children's early years of learning. The idea was to facilitate early language acquisition for children as they associated a specific language with a specific caregiver. The rationale for fostering the home language for young children included the need to maintain family ties, especially between grandparents and children. Even when the home language was temporarily sacrificed on the advice of school authorities, the family's goal was to ensure communication among the generations. The home language and cultural gifts were viewed as enhancing the children's school achievement and sense of self.

The idea of instilling cultural pride within the family as well as within the ecological context of the community was prevalent among bilingual families in Steel Town. Families were actively involved in the educational needs of their children, providing them with enriching experiences and activities. Family-shared activities included community festivities, visits to local attractions, church attendance, and trips to nearby cities, and, when possible, to Puerto Rico. The families saw a need for children to gain a sense of history and cultural knowledge in order to attain self-confidence in a social environment that shows little appreciation for children's linguistic and cultural gifts. This idea about a healthy sense of self appeared to be an attempt to provide children the necessary tools to survive in a community that devalues languages and cultures.

"Putting children first" is a slogan repeatedly voiced in the debates on the needs of children in America. Bilingual families in this study demonstrated their willingness to put their children at the center of the family's agenda. Busy professional families indicated that their children's needs were the number one priority in their personal and professional lives. Within the family domain and within the family context, every possible resource was used to benefit children.

Families used their political voice and collaborative power to advocate for the community while demonstrating a variety of coping strategies. These strategies were an integral part of the political struggle during the bilingual controversy. The collaborative power base modeled by the families was in sharp contrast to the larger community's coercive power tactics. My participant observations at educational events and school meetings showed how the oppressed families struggled and coped in a hostile climate imposed by the community.

First, the practice of "swallowing hard" to remain quiet was used historically in the community. The senior members of Steel Town relied on "swallowing hard" (*tragamos y tragamos*) as their primary strategy, believing that future generations would benefit from this approach. This strategy was in place for over twenty years, but did not enhance the educational opportunities for bilingual children in the community. This approach helped the mainstream community regard Latino families as the "quiet ones" and encouraged the community's oppressive tactics.

Second, coercive power structures silenced the voices of families struggling for quality school programs. The school board disregarded petitions, speeches, letters, and media appeals from children, families, and educators on issues. This strategy angered and disillusioned families, creating a climate of oppression for bilingual families. The mainstream power brokers felt justified in their beliefs and continued to perpetuate xenophobia.

Third, families initiated communications with the oppressors. The bilingual families reached out to the politically powerful by initiating meetings, offering media opportunities, and conducting door-to-door campaigns. Support and alliances with Anglo families were solicited throughout the community as well as through the local teachers' union. Awards and words of praise were bestowed on selected Anglo leaders, hoping to convince the community of the bilingual families' goodness and worth.

Fourth, selected Latino families sided with the oppressors. A kind of hegemony described by McLaren (1994) was evidenced when the powerful won the consent of a handful of the oppressed. The Latino leader who sided with the English-only advocates and was later appointed to the school board serves as a provocative example.

Fifth, families indicated solidarity by collaborating. The hundreds of like-minded families who joined together in order to ensure their children a quality education were documented in the media. The families reached out to all sectors of the community and found support from other Latino families, bilingual educators, religious leaders, community leaders, state educational leaders, nationally prominent bilingual leaders, and advocacy-minded organizations. The minister's congregation praying before a school board meeting is testimony to the bilingual families' attempts to generate wide community support. The collaborative spirit was historically significant yet seen by the larger community as a "Latino issue."

Sixth, the bilingual families assumed an attitude of patient expectation. A spirit of optimism was evident at the outset of a "let's wait and see" attitude, which became one of discouragement and disillusionment after it became evident that signing petitions, voicing their concerns to the community, press, and school board, and offering prayerful pleas would be disregarded.

Seventh, families demonstrated educational assertiveness. The bilingual families resorted to legal measures in their struggle for a quality education for their children. The Office of Civil Rights was notified of the issues impacting the education of bilingual children in Steel Town. The Puerto Rican Legal Defense Fund was also made aware of the existing educational conditions affecting Latino/a children.

Finally, Latino/a leaders showed a willingness to run for political office. Five bilingual leaders ran for political positions, including school board and city council positions, soon after the bilingual program was dismantled. Their failure to win these positions reflects the fact that current voting districts do not afford bilingual families a voice in the political process as they continue to be outnumbered, outvoted, and outmaneuvered. Will equitable representation ever be achieved in Steel Town?

What can schools do? The *consejos* and wisdom bilingual families imparted to the schools were congruent with the academic and cognitive advantages of bilingual education documented in the research literature. In addition, the families called for a shift from paradigms of shame to paradigms of compassion. The overview of bilingual education research provided in chapter 1 highlights findings that bilingualism is not detrimental to children's growth and development but does in fact provide an enriching learning opportunity. The advice provided the school by families interviewed in this study also supports the findings of Lucas, Henze, and Donato (1991), who present the features of high schools that promote the achievement of language-minority students.

Lucas et al.'s research illustrates how language minority students benefit in high schools where: (1) value is placed on the students' languages and cultures; (2) high expectations of language minority students are made concrete; (3) school leaders make the education of language-minority students a priority; (4) staff development is explicitly designed to help language-minority students more effectively; (5) a variety of courses and programs are offered; (6) the counseling program gives special attention to language-minority students; (7) parents of language-minority students are encouraged to become involved; and (8) staff members share a strong commitment to empower language-minority students (1991, 464–65).

The advice directed to the Steel Town schools by the bilingual families interviewed for this study encourages a deliberate shift from paradigms of shame to paradigms of compassion. This *consejos* from Agueybana families urges the school to :

1. Implement programs that can preserve home languages and cultures
2. Integrate caring and humanistic approaches
3. Accept the fact that institutions of learning are not the only knowledge brokers
4. Model ways of encouraging "linguistic and cultural integrity"
5. Initiate mentoring relationships

6. Interact and communicate in ways that value the attributes of diverse populations
7. Provide access to quality programs
8. Provide ethical and knowledgeable advice

First, the families expressed the need for schools to assist in preserving languages and cultures. An education capable of keeping home languages and cultures intact was viewed as a means of enhancing intergenerational communication among bilingual families. This advice is supported by decades of research in the field of bilingual education, including NABE's No Cost Study, which obtained quantitative data from over 1,200 families across the nation (see Wong Fillmore 1991). The ability to implement a program that emphasizes home languages and cultures will indicate to children that they no longer need to shed linguistic and cultural family knowledge in order to "fit in" with existing societal norms. Children should be allowed to shed the shame they have experienced in Steel Town and replace it with pride. Children enriched in this manner can continue to add to their existing repertoire of knowledge.

The families in this study expressed ongoing and long-standing painful experiences because of ignorance, intolerance, and racism. If schools implemented a caring curriculum, the families reasoned, then perhaps the child-centered approach modeled at home would help provide academic, psychological, and social benefits to the children. A caring and humanistic approach would assure that children would no longer be recipients of rejection, but recipients of a caring attitude reflecting positive human attributes.

The families indicated that schools are not the only knowledge brokers. Families have a wealth of information and wisdom they can share with schools. The bilingual families interviewed often indicated more knowledge about the literature and the research than the teachers and administrators responsible for educating their children. The families attempted to share their educational knowledge with school personnel, but this information was largely ignored.

These families modeled ways of allowing children to develop self-confidence and self-respect by affording a home learning environment that maintained an atmosphere of what they referred to as "linguistic and cultural integrity." Not only was linguistic and cultural knowledge imparted to children within the bilingual family structure, but it was shared with the community at large as gifts are shared with friends and relatives.

Bilingual families developed mentoring relationships in the community like those that they had experienced during their formative high school and college years. The idea that non-Latino mentors were willing to reach out and offer meaningful information underscored the fact that a path to educational success was possible for Latino/as. Providing bilingual students with very specific training, information, monitoring, and guidance regarding college applications was crucial for their college admission and retention.

It is universally recognized that all human beings long to be valued and appreciated. Yet the stories of pain revealed in this study show that schools need to evaluate their current modes of interaction and communication with linguistically and culturally diverse children to meet those basic human needs. Anglo-centered, detached ways of interacting are sending messages to Latino/a children that are being internalized as messages of rejection rather than acceptance. Intentional or unintentional, implicit or explicit, these messages and ways of interacting need to be reexamined and viewed in light of the needs expressed by language-minority informants. Educational climates of neglect are not helpful for the development of children or a democratic nation. The school climate and learning environment need to reflect a desire for the healthy development of members of our society.

The daily realities families experienced in Steel Town indicate a climate less than hospitable for bilingual children. The community context reflected an oppressive stance that was in turn mirrored in the educational experiences of the families in this study. Access and quality programs for all children in the "mythical" America is an educational, civil, and human right. Legal mandates in our nation may not be sufficient to protect children's educational civil rights, nor as in this case, the political will and voices of bilingual families. Coercive forces of power continued to exacerbate xenophobic perspectives that have effectively foreclosed the Latino/a children's opportunity to participate in a bilingual program.

The first bilingual teacher ever hired by the Steel Town school district is now retired. She shared the historical evolution of the district's bilingual program with me and reflected on the dismantling of the program. According to Mrs. Martinez, the State Department of Education had to step in repeatedly in 1964, 1970, and 1973 to encourage the school board to accept federally approved funding. In addition, the state was forced to examine the misplacement of bilingual students in special education classes. Mrs. Martinez was hired as a bilingual specialist in 1970; in the next two decades, additional personnel were hired and a bilingual vocational program was initiated with federal funds. The recent bilingual controversy was especially difficult for Mrs. Martinez:

> Why was the program dismantled? I think it was the numbers. . . . A growth from seven hundred to two thousand becomes a threat and a competition. The Hispanic group is interested in conserving the language. We have no one in positions of power, e.g., the school board. No one else fought for our rights, e.g., non-Latino parents. . . . The teacher's union never defended the program nor the teachers. Professor Diaz was fired from the community college. The superintendent and three school board members sit on that governing board. . . . We have no political clout. There is no redistricting here.

The family wisdom and power issues in this study can be viewed within the context of the complex interrelationships of language and culture in America. The families attempted to have their voices and their children's voices heard in a variety of ways. The victims combined passive and assertive coping strategies and options, yet the more powerful continued to impose their will. The educational needs of bilingual and bicultural children and families were sacrificed in the process.

The book entitled *Hold Your Tongue* by James Crawford (1992) documents the evolution of a national mood that helps perpetuate xenophobic views within the context of a historically diverse nation. How can bilingual families' struggle for a quality education be heard or understood by a nation that so values monolingualism and monoculturalism? Who stands to win when children continue to feel that schools and communities devalue the language and culture of their families? Who stands to win when schools continue to shortchange bilingual children? Who stands to win when children's talents, family wisdom, cultural knowledge, and linguistic knowledge are disregarded and ignored?

Linguistically and culturally diverse families have a tendency to think that advice imparted by educators is the law of the land. They may follow such advice even when it counters their own needs, values, and intuition. The idea of imposing English only at home needs to be abandoned. This advice is hurting the family's ability to communicate. Ethical educational practices tell us that healthy modes of interaction will assure that children are able to obtain the rich wisdom imparted by elders. This may appear to be a simplistic notion to some, yet at a time when children in our nation are referred to as "at risk" (rather than promising), their healthy sense of self appears crucial.

The role teachers play in the education of language-minority learners is critical for the future educational success of all learners. Colleges of education in our nation need to carefully consider how to best implement course work and experiences that will prepare teachers for informed decision making about quality educational programs. The stakes are high for children who are so unlike their teachers. Mrs. Martinez noted the importance of teacher education when she stated:

> It is up to the institutions of higher education (IHEs) to show commitment and to intensify their programs. Teachers are the soul of educational programs. IHEs need to see that competencies in cultural and linguistic diversity are strong so that teachers are prepared to deal better with our populations.

Mrs. Martinez's notion of teachers as the soul of educational programs points to the need to strengthen teacher education programs. Margarita said that she felt sorry for her teacher because she detected her helpless feeling about teaching second-language speakers. The need for collaborative power models that include teachers, students, and families is underscored by Antonia Darder:

If public schools are to provide successfully for the educational needs of bicultural students, they must work in collaboration with bicultural educators, students, parents, and their communities. Anything short of this effort suggests an educational process that is in danger of oppressing and disempowering students of color. This is not to imply that all teachers in bicultural communities must necessarily be teachers of color, but rather to emphasize that it is an arrogant and patronizing gesture for educators from the dominant culture to think that they can meet the needs of a culturally different community when they fail to work in solidarity with educators and other members of that community. (Darder 1991, 121)

A local religious leader shared his vision of solidarity and added humor to the discussions when he stated:

I grew up in a Polish household and learned Spanish in the seminary with many field experiences. I learned *atrevimiento*—daringness and willingness to make mistakes, so language became natural. Do you know what they call someone who speaks three languages? Trilingual. Do you know what they call someone who speaks two languages? Bilingual. Do you know what they call someone who speaks one language? American.

The English-only movement is a fear, a defensiveness. But many lament that they did not learn the language of their ancestors. Hispanics are asked to translate all the time by many agencies. When my grandparents came to America, they picked up a shovel and did not need the knowledge that is needed today. The job applications are technical. . . . It is more complex now. The dropout rates are high and the kids' identity and self-image are fragile.

Children don't need any more barriers, language. The school board rejected the report from its own study group. There is so much injustice in this situation.

We need coalitions . . . both religious and nonreligious.

While it is clear that this community context and this particular slice of history are unique, there is also evidence pointing to the educational neglect of bilingual children throughout America. Gandara (1994) notes how some of the recent educational reform initiatives mention foreign language study, yet "with the exceptions of the Berman Weiler report, none makes mention of the possibility of nurturing the language skills that America's students bring to the classroom" (48). Gandara indicates how the reform movement has been "conspicuously silent" on the advantages of primary language instruction, and how teachers might adapt curricula to meet the needs of diverse students, including second-language speakers.

Additional questions come to mind when I recall the bilingual parish begging the Steel Town school board, excited bilingual families signing petitions and hoping that once, just this once, their voices would be heard. Unprecedented political campaigns were launched. Children's voices eloquently filled the school board meetings with requests for a quality bilingual program. All these activities continue to beg power-related questions such as: Is the American Dream for monolinguals only? What will it take to have children's voices heard?

Why is it important to be knowledgeable about languages and cultures? The nations of the world have indicated interest in communicating readily and easily via newly evolving information highways for a variety of purposes. Our generation is actively seeking to improve avenues of communication to enhance our economic possibilities as well as the well-being and the future of the Planet. Language learning is clearly knowledge that will benefit our citizens as we attempt to organize, understand, communicate, and plan for future cross-cultural and global possibilities.

The President's Commission on Foreign Language and International Studies (1980) stated:

> The United States is blessed with a largely untapped resource of talent in the form of racial and ethnic minorities who, by being brought into the mainstream of educational and employment opportunities in the areas of foreign language and international studies, can be expected to make rapid, new, and valuable contributions to America's capacity to deal persuasively and effectively with the world outside its borders. (24)

Most nations have included second-language learning opportunities for children. Second- and multiple-language learning is common: Danish schools' educational system includes compulsory second-language learning at age eleven; Swedish schools initiate second-language learning in the lower grades; France is initiating language learning for children under five; three-year-olds in the northern parts of Germany are experimenting with second-language learning; Hungarian nursery schools are introducing second languages; Italy affords seven-year-olds an opportunity to learn English, French, Spanish, or German; Greece is extending a program initiated in 1987 to all primary schools (eight- to nine-year-olds); Luxembourg children learn German and French in the elementary school; teachers in Luxembourg are expected to be competent in German, French, English, and Letzeburgesch; England includes French, German, Italian, and Spanish in the elementary curriculum; a national project in Scotland includes French, German, Spanish, and Italian (Peck 1993); Canada and Australia have official policies favoring bilingualism.

In American schools, bilingual education continues to be suspect. Bilingualism, bilingual education, and bicultural populations have been historically viewed as deficient, dispensable, and devalued. The legislative advances addressing issues of equity in the 1960s and 1970s have not alleviated the current xenophobic perspectives for either bilingual or potentially bilingual children. Our nation faces a bleak future of miseducation, continued language loss, economic uncertainty, racial tension and conflict, and an uncertain impact on international peacekeeping activities.

The need to reclaim cultural and linguistic losses is dictated by the needs of children in our communities and in our society. American schools, implicitly and explicitly, encourage the loss of home languages. From the child's point of view, it is clear that you are expected to shed your family language and culture in order to be "acceptable" in mainstream society. If you can wait long enough, when you reach high school, however, you are permitted to learn preselected second languages. The results are not impressive. How many persons can boast about their high school language proficiency? How many children speak the home language of their grandparents?

The bilingual families interviewed in this study represent the many "success stories" that our schools can encourage. It was evident that their voices were silenced. Yet, if the larger community had listened to their wisdom and advice, they would have realized that the strategies advocated by bilinguals would lead to additional contributions to their community. If we could multiply the contributions of these families to Steel Town by the potential talents and gifts present in schools, perhaps we could envision a greater Steel Town and a stronger democratic nation. The coercive power structure that dimmed the light being shed by bilingual families on education also deprived itself of knowledge about how to best support the needs of children. Ultimately, the oppressive climate will only continue to have cumulative and devastating effects on a community that has been historically valued for its cultural and linguistic diversity. The children should not have to carry the shame.

Are American schools and communities willing to implement collaborative power models? Should the schools of a democratic nation insist that children's languages and cultures be valued? Are collaborative models with bicultural families appropriate democratic choices for schools to pursue? How can communities take greater responsibility for initiating collaborative process models? How can communities assure that children's linguistic and cultural gifts are valued so they can implement paradigms of pride?

The educational transformation model advocated by Freire (1993) would be valuable to communities like Steel Town. Such a model advocates initiating grassroots educational efforts with families, teachers, and specialists. The ability and willingness to democratize, decentralize, and divest excessive and abusive power will ultimately determine the types of quality programs children will receive in Steel Town and in the nation. Mehan's advice seems appropriate: "We must find ways to take progressive political action without giving into the politics of despair, or we will be trapped in the infinite regression of nihilism which renders actions impossible" (1994, 92).

The ability of schools and communities to view themselves as co-workers with families and teachers will transform the coercive power structure currently oppressing and dominating language-minority populations. In spite of the hidden and not so hidden English-only curriculum that has continued to perpetuate a Carlisle school mentality in our schools, the challenge for the new millennium will be to explore and implement collaborative power models that can restore the losses to bilingual families, children, schools, and communities. Instead of hearing Margarita say, "En esta escuela no se habla Español," we may hear her say that languages and cultures are valued in her school. Instead of hearing students express their helplessness like "lions in a cage, and then you put in a little goat," we may hear about schools that are caring and compassionate.

Ferdman notes, "When a group perceives that its cultural features compare favorably with those of other groups, it should come to hold more positive images of itself. If, on the other hand, features central to the group's cultural identity are viewed negatively in the larger society, the group will probably incorporate a negative component in its self evaluation" (1991, 356).

Persons with stereotypical notions about families as being uncaring about their children's educational future have not met the bilingual families in Steel Town, the bilingual families in Lowell, Massachussetts (Crawford 1992), or the families of the Foundation Center in California. When early childhood education centers in California were attacked by bureaucrats recently, Latino families participated in a hunger strike (Lopez 1995). Linguistically and culturally diverse parents care a great deal about their children's education.

To the high school principal who shared how blatant and acceptable racism has become by stating, "This is America!" I will say that many of us will resist being a part of such an oppressive America. Our schoolchildren are taught about a different America, an America that promises democracy, freedom, and equal educational opportunities. Where is our democratic America? Where is the America so many of us long for? So many families in America pin their hopes on educational equity and freedom for their children, as they dream the American Dream.

The lives of the participants in this study have continued to evolve, as have events relating to the education of language-minority children in the community. My attempts to ascertain the status of the civil rights complaint submitted by Latino/a leaders in Steel Town received this response from the Office of Civil Rights: "due to the voluminous information collected and the complexity of the issues raised in this case, review of the information gathered in the investigation has been more time-consuming than was originally anticipated" (September 1994).

Latino/a leaders in the community, including two of the "success stories" interviewed for this study, found that events leading to the bilingual controversy directly impacted their professional careers. Professor Diaz, an outspoken community advocate who led the action to submit the complaint to the Office of Civil Rights, found that his faculty position at a local institution of higher learning was not renewed. Latino families wondered whether the fact that the local school superintendent serves on the governing board of the same institution was related to Professor Diaz's situation.

The school district's coordinator of bilingual education, who had worked with the Bilingual Education Committee and supported the twenty-year-old bilingual program, requested a transfer to another position in the district. The strain of the political struggle deeply affected the coordinator personally. As a vital leader in her community, this professional sought to stay in Steel Town where her family lives and where her child attends school. "My heart is not in it," she indicated, referring to the newly implemented immersion program. She preferred to work on behalf of the local district in a different administrative capacity.

Transfers of clergy active in the bilingual controversy took place. I cannot say whether their moves were by personal choice or decided by their religious leaders. The Latino minister who led the prayer of petition before the school board at the January meeting moved to another state. A non-Latino minister who advocated on behalf of the bilingual families moved to another community.

A local priest highly esteemed by the bilingual families was also transferred from his parish to a nearby community. The local newspaper referred to this priest as a "mover, a shaker" and reported that "At the mention of this last effort . . . a curtain of weariness falls over the priest. He [the priest] noted that voting by South Side

Hispanics reached its peak with the election of the district justice in 1991. . . . Since then the Hispanic vote withered, culminating in last year's primaries when five Latinos ran for school board and City Council and were [all] defeated" (M. Floyd Hall, 1994).

The three bilingual teachers who left the school district in 1993 indicated that their reason for leaving was the school's decision to eliminate the bilingual program. One teacher decided to pursue a doctoral degree. The two other teachers returned to Puerto Rico. Interestingly enough, nearby Post Town school administrators traveled to Puerto Rico to recruit bilingual teachers in the Spring of 1995. The remaining bilingual teachers of Steel Town were reassigned throughout the district and told to teach English only.

A newly arrived high school senior from Puerto Rico in the fall of 1994 was retained a grade by the Steel Town school due to lack of language proficiency. The local attorney representing the student asked the school district,

> Is there a policy in the Steel Town School District which prohibits matriculation of a student into the appropriate grade based solely on limited English proficiency? If so, I would appreciate receiving a copy of the policy. Also, who makes decisions regarding student placement and on what legal basis is such a decision made? (August 15, 1994)

The student initiated a legal action with the assistance of the Puerto Rican Legal Defense Fund. This case never reached the courts as the district complied with the student's request for appropriate grade level placement.

An English-only city ordinance was passed in the fall of 1994 in the city of Post Town. Petitions with 2,029 signatures were gathered by the Latino/a leadership and presented to the city mayor. One of the city council members stated that the leader presenting the petition "should become a principal in Puerto Rico and lead the challenge of teaching the young children to speak English." The petitioners called the English-only ordinance "an expression of nativism, historically the reaction of intolerant residents toward new immigrants." The petitioners asked if Post Town resembled Nazi Germany of the 1930s where Jews were not welcome.

At this writing South Side children were bused and entered in the school district's immersion program. The newly elected school board (1994–95) still had no language minority or minority citizens. The school superintendent continued to obtain salary increases and positive yearly reviews.

The school board voted to demolish and rebuild a school on the West Side of Steel Town. There were no new schools for the South Side children. The West Side monolingual parents were not willing to support the bilingual families or to build alliances with them. One parent from the West Side school met me in a hallway and whispered, "You understand why we could not help with the bilingual program!"

Actually, I have a real hard time understanding. I ask, How long will the privileged children of Steel Town be more valued than the bicultural children?

Eight of the "success stories" bilingual professional families continue to reside in Steel Town. Four of the families left the community and are currently contributing as leaders to communities elsewhere. Maria Rivera, the high school student who provided leadership for her peers, is currently attending the Pennsylvania State University.

The xenophobic mentality continues in Steel Town as the local housing authority released a language policy, stating,

> Those of us who speak another language must understand that when we speak in an unfamiliar tongue we leave an air of discomfort with those among us who don't understand. As a matter of fact it is regarded as rudeness. It is suggested that English be recognized as the language to be used by all of us. (April 29, 1994)

It is interesting to note that the *Yniquez v. Mofford* decision (730 F. Supp. 309 D. Ariz.) bars an English-only rule by a government entity on the grounds that it violates the First Amendment.

In a letter to the regional civil rights director, one of the local attorneys summed up the feelings of the families waiting to hear from the Office of Civil Rights:

> While the allegations of discrimination set forth in the complaint remain unresolved and new issues arise, we remain in "limbo" while waiting for our government to respond to the needs of its citizens. Neither budget cuts nor reductions in personnel can justify the relegation of minority students to the conditions which are the subject of the complaint. (November 11, 1994)

APPENDIX A

Bilingual Program Recommendations
Submitted by the Bilingual Committee

1. INTRODUCTION

A committee composing the School District teachers, administrators, and community representatives has been meeting since January 1992 to review, discuss, and deliberate various facets of the district's bilingual program and to prepare recommendations for the program's future. Since there is a need to determine if changes in the bilingual program would impact space needs in the district, the committee is issuing this report to address primarily that concern and those related to it. Each recommendation herein represents a vote of the majority of the committee. In future months, the committee will review additional issues, such as the identification and placement of students into the various phases of the program. It is anticipated that these concerns will not impact space needs.

The early sections of this report provide background information on bilingual programs in general as well as one school district that remains anonymous.

2. DEFINITION OF TERMS

This section on specialized vocabulary and its meaning in bilingual programs is included as an aid to understanding this report.

Bilingual – refers to knowledge and use of two languages.

Bilingual Instructional Program – refers to the use of two languages, one of which is English, to teach subject matter. This term also applies to the program for all limited English proficient students.

Dominance – refers to the language most often used by the student for communication and self-expression.

ESOL – English for Speakers of Other Languages. Same as ESL. This is also the name of one phase of the bilingual program.

ESL – English as a Second Language. Usually refers to the teaching of English to persons whose native language is other than English.

Immersion – a program which serves students with limited English proficiency wherein children learn a second language through content and instruction in that language.

LEP – Limited English Proficient - the term used to describe students who speak a language other than English and who have not yet fully mastered English in its oral and written forms.

L-Core – the Area School District's assessment center for limited English proficient students; it stands for Language, Communication and Resource Center.

Maintenance Bilingual Program – a structured sequential educational program in two languages throughout the school experience of the student. A maintenance bilingual program may serve both non-English dominant and English dominant students or only non-English dominant students.

Native Language – the first language learned by a child, usually the language of his/her home.

Primary Language – the first language learned by a child, usually the language of his/her home and most often used to express ideas and concepts.

Submersion – "sink or swim" process in which limited English proficient students receive no special instruction. The U.S. Supreme Court ruled in 1974 in the Lau vs. Nichols case that submersion violates federal civil rights law.

TBE – Transitional Bilingual Education Program - a program which serves students who are limited English proficient; it provides for instruction in the student's home/primary language and English until the student is able to function effectively in classes conducted in English. This is the kind of program the School District has in grades K–8.

3. THE LAW AND BILINGUAL EDUCATION

The law regarding bilingual education and its implementation in the public schools is based on the Civil Rights Act of 1964. The case having greatest impact on the direction of bilingual education in the United States is the Supreme Court decision of Lau vs. Nichols in 1974. In this decision, it was held that the Civil Rights Act of 1964 required schools to give extra help to students who do not speak English. However, the Court never stipulated the type of extra help required. Some states have mandated bilingual programs; Pennsylvania has not.

However, in 1986, Pennsylvania adopted a set of guidelines based on Title 22, Chapter 5, Section 5.6(b) of the state Curriculum Regulations. The introduction to the guidelines states:

> Each school district shall provide for a program for each student whose dominant language is not English for the purpose of facilitating English proficiency. Such programs may include bilingual/bicultural or English as a Second Language (ESL) curriculum. (PDE 1986)

Additionally, Section 1703(f) of the Equal Educational Opportunity Act of 1974

(EEOA) has generally been interpreted by the courts as requiring that school districts take effective action to overcome language barriers by providing a means of equal access. That action may be either bilingual education or ESL support.

4. BILINGUAL EDUCATION RESEARCH

After the Supreme Court ruled that school districts had to give extra help to students who do not speak English, a task force, mandated by the Supreme Court, drew up guidelines for "educational approaches which would constitute appropriate 'affirmative steps' to be taken by a noncomplying school district 'to open up its instructional program.'" These guidelines became known as the *Lau remedies*. One of the remedies, which went beyond what the Supreme Court had mandated, required bilingual education for elementary-school children who spoke little or no English. Even though this remedy had no legal status, for all practical purposes it became the accepted practice in many school districts nationally. This remedy resulted in what is usually called a transitional bilingual program, a program that uses the native language while a transition to English is gradually accomplished.

Until the middle 1980s, Title VII federal funds for programs for limited English proficient students went almost exclusively to districts that used instruction in the native language of the students. It is from these funded programs that most research came. Thus, little research was conducted in this country on "structured immersion" programs. Structured immersion is usually described as an approach that uses English as the language of instruction, but uses bilingual teachers so that concepts can be explained in the native language, when necessary.

The major question that research has tried to answer is what language should be used for instruction. Proponents for all sides on this issue can find research to support their position. James Crawford, in the April 1, 1987 issue of *Education Week*, quoted two federal Education Department researchers who concluded after a review of the research that:

> The case for the effectiveness of transitional bilingual education is so weak that exclusive reliance on this instructional method is clearly not justified. Too little is known about the problems of educating language minorities to prescribe a specific remedy at the federal level. . . . Each school district should decide what type of special program is most appropriate for its own unique setting.

In the same issue, Crawford also states the following:

> Among educators, the word is getting out: Children who begin school without English can thrive in well-designed programs that build on their native-language skills. Increasingly, researchers are documenting the benefits of bilingual methodologies in promoting academic development at no cost to the acquisition of English. Politically,

however, bilingual education has never been more vulnerable. It is a prime target of the burgeoning "English-only" movement, which opposes bilingual services on ideological grounds, arguing that they impede the assimilation of new immigrants and threaten to divide Americans along language lines.

As can be seen from these two quotes, there is wide divergence of opinions on the "best" program.

5. HISTORY OF THE BILINGUAL PROGRAM IN THE AREA SCHOOL DISTRICT

The Bilingual Program in the School District began in 1971, shortly after the employment of the first Coordinator of Bilingual and Minority Education. The program provided native language instruction for students recently arrived from Puerto Rico, with little or no English speaking skills. Only a small percentage of the total Latino population participated in this program, which was located at an Elementary, a Junior High, and a High School. After the closing of the School, the program was moved to be continued at three sites through most of the 1970's.

During the 1977–78 school year, a decision was made to expand the elementary program to two additional sites and instruction was in both Spanish and English, classes were self-contained, and students in those classes ranged in level from kindergarten through grade six. By this time, the bilingual program had two phases: bilingual, which used native language instruction; and transitional, which used mostly English for instruction. In 1984, bilingual program students moved to either phase.

By the mid 1980's, native language instruction at the high school level was eliminated. Because of inequities caused by limited grouping options, concerns were raised about the elementary and middle school program. As a result, in 1988 the administration recommended the reconfiguration of the two elementary centers. Bilingual students in grades K–2 were sent to one center; bilingual students in grades 3–5 moved to another center that provided an increased equitable delivery of services by providing more placement options, and it minimized the movement of students within the district. Also during this year, the bilingual program evolved into its current three phases. For the 1992–93 school year, the middle school bilingual location was expanded to include a second site at another school.

The bilingual program in the district has grown as the number of Hispanic students has increased. In 1971, 6.6% of the district's population was Hispanic compared to 21% in 1992. It is interesting to note that while the total student population decreased during this period, the Hispanic population grew noticeably. This growth has been gradual as noted below:

Year	Total District Enrollment	Total Hispanic Enrollment	Percentage of Hispanic Students
1971	17,286	1,150	6.6%
1973	16,925	1,320	7.8%
1977	14,235	1,461	10.3%
1988	11,720	1,969	16.8%
1992	12,684	2,720	21.4%

6. DESCRIPTION OF THE PRESENT PROGRAM

As of October 28, 1992, the bilingual program was serving 1,168 limited English proficient students from grades K–12 who speak twenty different languages. Spanish is the native language of 1,101 students (94.2%) with the remaining 67 students speaking 19 different languages. The students whose native language is Spanish receive a program in grades K–8 that includes instruction in their native language, if appropriate to meet the needs of the student. At the high school level, limited English proficient students whose native language is Spanish receive all instruction in English. The limited English proficient students whose native language is not Spanish receive instruction in English at all levels. Since there are variations in program by level for students whose native language is Spanish, each will be described separately.

ELEMENTARY

The present elementary program for native Spanish speakers consists of three phases: Primary Language Instruction (PLI), Sheltered English (SE) and regular program with English for Speakers of Other Languages (ESOL) support. Students enter the program at an appropriate phase, depending upon facility with English, and are not required to go through all phases. Each phase has the following characteristics:

Primary Language Instruction (PLI)

- teaches all academic subjects in Spanish
- provides instruction in English for Speakers of Other Languages (ESOL) thirty to 100 minutes per week
- requires instruction in specialist subjects, such as art and music, in English
- provides multi-cultural activities, as well as the maintenance of Latino culture through varied classroom activities

- parallels the content of subjects in the regular program
- needs approximately three to four years to complete
- groups students throughout the day with other students in the PLI phase

Sheltered English (SE)

- teaches all classes in English with a teacher who is fluent in Spanish so concept clarification can be in the native language
- includes daily instruction in ESOL
- teaches academic subjects the same as in the regular program, but modifies instructional techniques and the level of English used to accommodate students learning English as a second language
- provides for multi-cultural activities, as well as the maintenance of Latino culture through varied classroom activities
- groups students throughout the day with other students in the SE phase
- needs approximately one to two years to complete

English for Speakers of Other Languages (ESOL)

- places students in regular program classes, but provides specialized instruction for the acquisition of English, reading and writing skills several times a week
- needs approximately one to two years to complete

The PLI and SE phases are offered at two sites. one site for the bilingual program students in grades kindergarten through second and the second site through fifth graders. Students who need PLI or SE, regardless of their home school, attend one of the two centers. Until recently students in the ESOL phase were also served at these centers. However, during the 1991–92 school year, the district began providing the ESOL phase at the home school and has continued this practice.

Students whose native language is not Spanish receive the ESOL phase described above at their home school. This phase may be provided by the reading teacher if only one or two students in the school need assistance. If there are more students in need of service, an itinerant ESOL teacher visits the school to provide support. Tutorial support in the native language is provided for students who are adjusting to English only classrooms, if necessary and where possible.

MIDDLE SCHOOL

The middle school program has the same three phases described for the elementary school program. Until this school year, the program was located at one school. However, effective this year, the program is split between two schools. In addition to its own students, one school will serve students who need any phase of the program. Students in the ESOL phase who began instruction at one school, are continuing their instruction at that school so a change in middle school assignment does not become necessary. This year they are able to offer the phases of the program by grade level; and all students who need PLI or SE are grouped together by grade.

Students whose native language is not Spanish receive the ESOL phase at either of the Middle Schools.

HIGH SCHOOL

At the high school level all instruction is in English with the goal to have students proficient enough in English so they can participate in the regular offerings of the high school. The original design of the English for Speakers of Other Languages (ESOL) program at the High School was that of three levels of ESOL instruction. A student remained at each level for a period of one academic year and then advanced into the next level. A student entering the ESOL level one in ninth grade would not be able to take advantage of the regular course offerings until the twelfth grade. Some students, however, were still not at a level of English competency after the three years to handle regular classes and thus still required additional ESOL instruction.

In order to better meet the needs of all students the school recently made revisions to the program. For those students who are in need of an additional year of ESOL instruction, an ESOL 4 class has been added. The new design also includes an accelerated program enabling a student to virtually move through any number of the levels within a shortened period of time, perhaps as short as one and one-half to two years. This can occur by moving a student into a higher ESOL level within an academic year, or skipping a level at the end of a year. At level four this accelerated group of students takes an ESOL class called Transitional 4, which is literature based and develops deeper thinking skills as well as refining writing skills. The purpose of this class is to better prepare the students to enter a college prep track. Students who show potential and have the desire to enter mainstream programs are encouraged to do so at a time when they have demonstrated a level of English competency necessary to succeed in the mainstream courses.

Each level of this ESOL program has the following characteristics:

LEVEL 1: ESOL 1

- students have almost no level of English competency.
- ESOL classes include reading, composition, speaking and vocabulary development. One of the two credits given for the reading and composition courses is in lieu of one credit for social studies. Mathematics is taught by ESOL staff and personal typing is taken during the second semester.

Level 2: ESOL 2

- students have a limited working knowledge of English and have some difficulty expressing themselves in oral and/or written communication.
- students receive two classes daily of ESOL to develop oral and written skills.
- students receive math, science, social studies, and health instruction from ESOL staff.
- some advanced students at this level may begin to receive instruction in math and science in the regular program, with added tutorial support from ESOL staff.

Level 3: ESOL 3

- students can function confidently in some English speaking environments, but usually do not know enough English to deal with the reading and writing demands of the regular program.
- students acquiring English quickly begin to take additional classes (English, math, science and social studies) in the regular program.
- ESOL classes in the major subjects are provided for students who are not yet at a level of competency which permits them to function satisfactorily in the regular program.

Level 4: ESOL 4 and Transitional (TRANS) 4

- students in the ESOL 4 classes are still in need of additional ESOL classes in the major subjects prior to entering all regular programs.
- the focus in ESOL 4 classes is the further development of reading, writing, vocabulary, and thinking skills.
- TRANS 4 is designed for those students who have the ability to work successfully in the regular program, but also have a need to broaden their reading, language and thinking skills.
- TRANS 4 students are encouraged to take regular English classes in addition to the TRANS 4 class.

7. CHARACTERISTICS FOR EACH PROGRAM PHASE

In order to assure that limited English proficient (LEP) students are placed in the most appropriate educational program upon entry or re-entry into the school district, an initial evaluation for placement is conducted in English, and Spanish when appropriate. Entry and exit criteria are established to reflect realistic levels of achievement as the students progress through each level of the multi-phase bilingual program. The district's Bilingual Education Program accommodates language minority limited English proficient students.

Each student is evaluated in the areas of oral language proficiency, reading and written language skills in order to determine his/her dominant language. After all testing has been completed and previous school records reviewed, an appropriate placement recommendation is made.

Follow-up assessment is conducted when a teacher determines that the student has achieved the necessary skills to move from one phase of the program to the next. Students in the various phases of the program display the following characteristics:

Students Entering the Primary Language Instruction Phase (K–8)

- student's dominant language is Spanish
- student is limited English proficient
- student may be a non-English speaker or limited English speaker
- student requires development of English language skills (reading, writing and speaking)
- Spanish is the language of the home
- literacy skills in Spanish (reading and writing) have been developed or are in the process of being developed
- student comes from a program where Spanish has been the primary language of instruction and student is non-English speaker/limited-English speaker

Students Entering the Sheltered English Phase (K–8)

- student's dominant language is Spanish
- student is limited English proficient
- student may be a limited English speaker or a fluent English speaker who needs to develop reading and writing skills in English
- continued development in English language skills is necessary
- Spanish is often the language of the home
- literacy skills may be stronger in Spanish but are also being developed in English
- concept clarification in Spanish is often necessary for effective cognitive academic learning

Students Entering the Regular Program with ESOL Support Phase (K–8)

- student may be fully bilingual
- student is limited English proficient and according to the tests is near the fluent English speaker
- student requires continued support to develop reading and writing skills in English
- student's prior schooling may have been in a bilingual setting and/or ESOL

Students Entering the Regular Education Program (K–8)

- student may be bilingual or a monolingual English speaker
- student's oral English proficiency is at mastery and he/she is a fluent English speaker
- student does not require ESOL support
- student may require English reading

Students Entering the ESOL Level 1 (High School)

- student's dominant language is other than English
- student is a non-English speaker or a limited English speaker
- student is non-English proficient and has almost zero level of English competency
- student requires intensive English language instruction in speaking, vocabulary development, reading and composition
- student's prior schooling may have been in a bilingual setting and/or ESOL

Students Entering the ESOL Level 2 (High School)

- student's dominant language is other than English
- student is a limited English speaker
- student has developed some basic competencies in English but is still limited English proficient
- student requires intensive English language instruction to develop oral, reading and writing skills
- student's prior schooling may have been in a bilingual setting and/or ESOL

Students Entering ESOL Level 3 (High School)

- student's dominant language is other than English
- student is a limited English speaker or a fluent English speaker
- student is still limited English proficient in reading and writing but has developed a level of competency in English that allows for participating in some English speaking environments
- student is in need of ESOL classes in the major subjects
- student's performance in English speaking, reading and writing may allow for participation in the regular program for some major subjects
- student's prior schooling may have been in a bilingual setting and/or ESOL

Students Entering the ESOL Level 4 (High School)

- student may be bilingual
- student is a fluent English speaker

- student needs further development in English reading and writing to attain English proficiency and improve competencies
- student is in need of ESOL classes in some major subject as he/she is still limited English proficient in reading or writing
- student is able to work in English alone for participation in some major subjects in the regular program
- student's prior schooling may have been in a bilingual setting and/or ESOL

Students Entering the ESOL Transitional Level 4 (High School)

- student may be bilingual
- student is a fluent English speaker
- student is still limited English proficient in reading and writing and needs TRANS 4 for refinement in English reading, writing, and thinking skills, all other classes are in the regular program
- student's prior school may have been in a bilingual setting and/or ESOL

8. BELIEF STATEMENTS

The Random House College Dictionary gives the following definition for *believe:* to have confidence in the truth or the reliability of something without absolute proof. Since there is no consensus among all researchers on the "best program," the recommendations found in the next section of this report are based upon the beliefs held by the committee members who prepared this report. These beliefs arise from within, and are an accumulation of our knowledge, professional training, experiences, and feelings.

The following beliefs apply to the entire K–12 program:

1. We believe the present program design is based upon accepted research.
2. We believe that the structure of the program provides challenges at all levels which guarantee success, build self-esteem, and further encourage students to strive for greater goals.
3. We believe that all students should become proficient in English.
4. We believe that acquisition of English proficiency, in addition to academics, significantly increases the learning task for limited English proficient students.
5. We believe that having a strong foundation in a native language promotes a smooth transition to learning in English.
6. We believe that what is learned in the native language can be transferred to English, not only in content area subjects, like science and mathematics, but also to skills in reading and writing.

7. We believe there are two levels of language proficiency: conversational and academic. Generally it takes one to three years to achieve conversational proficiency and an additional three to four years to achieve academic proficiency.
8. We believe that a student will be no more proficient in his second language than he is in his first language.
9. We believe that grouping students for the program is preferable to decentralizing students for instruction.

The following beliefs are the foundation of the elementary program:

10. We believe children build on prior knowledge developed in their native language; therefore, teaching children in their native language helps to build background knowledge which will empower them to succeed in school.
11. We believe that educating the child in the native language promotes positive self-esteem, enhances critical thinking, and helps prepare the child for participation in society.
12. We believe that one maximizes the potential for parental involvement when the language of instruction matches the home language.
13. We believe that native language instruction accelerates growth in areas such as reading, mathematics, and English language for second language learners as compared to limited English proficient students who have not used native language instruction.

The following belief is the foundation of the middle school program:

14. We believe that the middle school program should be a transitional period between the elementary and high school programs.

The following belief is for the high school program:

15. We believe that acquisition of English proficiency is a necessity which enhances a child's academic/vocational success during and after high school.

9. RECOMMENDATIONS

The bilingual committee thoroughly reviewed the various types of programs available to meet the needs of limited English proficient students. On a continuum, this review included programs that would have used English only to programs whose goals are to maintain the native language throughout grades K–12. This review resulted in the following recommendations:

RECOMMENDATION 1: PHILOSOPHY STATEMENT

The School District believes that it has the responsibility to provide an education for all children which prepares them as participants in the economic, political, and social community. Our Transitional Bilingual Education Program has been developed to provide for the needs of students acquiring English as a second language. By providing initial and supportive instruction in the primary language at selected grade levels while simultaneously introducing sequential oral and written English language skills, limited English proficient students will transfer their academic and cognitive skills from their primary language to English. The thrust of the program is to develop both cognitive and communication skills in the English language.

RECOMMENDATION 2: OBJECTIVES OF THE PROGRAM

1. To provide limited English proficient students with experiences which maintain proficiency in their primary language until students are able to meaningfully comprehend English as their language of instruction.
2. To build upon the initial knowledge and experiences of limited English proficient students.
3. To utilize the cultural diversity of limited English proficient students to enhance cultural sensitivity.
4. To provide support services for limited English proficient students with special needs comparable to those provided for students in the regular program.
5. To provide an educational environment which will help develop a positive self-image in limited English proficient students.
6. To increase sensitivity to the objectives of the bilingual program through inservice activities for all staff.
7. To provide bilingual counseling services for limited English proficient students.
8. To develop relationships between the home and school which will foster an understanding of the educational needs of the limited English proficient student.
9. To inform the educational community and the community at large of the objectives of the bilingual program.
10. To assess limited English proficient students continuously for academic and linguistic growth.
11. To periodically evaluate the effectiveness of the bilingual program.

RECOMMENDATION 3: ELEMENTARY SCHOOL PROGRAM

It is recommended that the program for the elementary grades remain as described earlier in this report.

RECOMMENDATION 4: MIDDLE SCHOOL PROGRAM

The middle school program should be the bridge between the elementary school program, which offers instruction in Spanish for students who need it, and the high school program, which offers instruction in English only. To accomplish this, it is recommended that the Primary Language Instruction be phased out in grades seven and eight and replaced with a transitional phase that starts in grade seven. In this new Transitional Language Phase, instruction would be provided for continued growth in reading, writing, and thinking skills in Spanish, for those students who need it. The present practice of providing instruction in science, social studies, and mathematics in Spanish would be eliminated; these subjects would be taught in English, with Spanish support. This means that out of forty-two instructional periods per six-day cycle, thirty-three would be in English: twelve periods for science and social studies where the main objective is to learn English through the use of science and social studies content with Spanish support where needed; six periods for mathematics, with Spanish support where needed; six periods for ESOL; and nine periods for related arts subjects such as music, physical education, and home economics. After completion of the Transitional Language phase, students would move to Sheltered English, where the instruction in reading, writing, and thinking skills will change from Spanish to English. It is also recommended that the present Spanish for Native Speakers course at School, which currently replaces part of the social studies curriculum, be eliminated contingent upon the foreign language curriculum revised to address the needs of native Spanish speakers who choose to take Spanish.

RECOMMENDATION 5: HIGH SCHOOL

It is recommended that the high school program remain as described earlier in this report.

RECOMMENDATION 6: CLASS SIZE

It is recommended that class size remain at the present ratio of 18 to 1 in the PLI and SE phases of the program, and the four phases at the high school level.

RECOMMENDATION 7: LOCATION

It is recommended that the present distribution of the elementary PLI and SE phases of the program into two centers by grade level be eliminated in favor of two centers that each serves grades K–S. It is further recommended that the PLI and SE phases of the program for middle school students continue to be offered at two centers and that the high school continue at one center. The ESOL phase of the program should continue to be delivered in the home school.

A center approach provides the most cost effective means to deliver the recommended programs and provides the widest range of services to limited English proficient students. Two K–S centers keep most of the elementary age limited English proficient students in one location during their elementary school years rather than the present system of two locations, each serving selected grade levels. Based on the district's history and current numbers, the two elementary schools that would house bilingual students would continue to be shown that the largest numbers of limited English proficient students are in these attendance areas. This, in turn, affects the transportation problems evident in our current configuration at the elementary level. Continuation of the programs at these schools is recommended because they are the home schools of the majority of the limited English proficient students.

It is also recommended that high school students who exit the bilingual program at the completion of grade nine or later be permitted to remain in high school until graduation if they choose to do so. The present practice requires the students to return to High School when they exit the program.

RECOMMENDATION 8: PARENT OPTIONS

It is recommended that parents who oppose the placement of their child in any phase of the program for limited English proficient students be permitted to request a team review of the placement. This team would consist of the parent, the receiving principal or designee, a representative from the office of minority education, and two teachers, one of whom must be a bilingual teacher. A nonvoting parent advocate is welcome as part of the discussion. The decision of this team would be binding.

RECOMMENDATION 9: PROGRAM EVALUATION

It is recommended that the district hire an outside researcher who has had experience evaluating bilingual programs to evaluate the district's bilingual program and that the bilingual committee be involved in the selection.

10. FUTURE COMMITTEE DELIBERATIONS

Because the program model serves as the basis of the bilingual education program, the first priority of this committee was to research and develop the model. However, there are a number of significant issues involving the delivery of the program model that still need to be addressed. They are: criteria for placement in the program, testing and tracking of progress throughout the program, the role of the district's language assessment center, and a system for quality control.

Children are initially placed in the program through referral to the Center. The Center then registers the student, administers testing, and determines the child's-placement. This process needs to be reviewed and recommendations submitted to the superintendent of schools for consideration.

The testing and tracking of students has been criticized for the length of time in moving students through each phase of the current program. The testing process and tracking of students need to be reviewed and recommendations submitted to the superintendent of schools for consideration.

The role of L-Core in communicating with building level educators, parents, and the community, as well as in the above processes, should be reviewed and redefined and recommendations submitted to the superintendent of schools for consideration.

An analysis of students' progress and achievements in bilingual education could be the basis of a study, which could shape the focus for the future of the program in the BASD.

STUDENT ENROLLMENT IN BILINGUAL EDUCATION
FOR THE 1992-93 SCHOOL YEAR

The following table lists students currently enrolled in phases of the district's bilingual program compared to the total student enrollment at each grade level:

Grade	Primary Language Instruction	Sheltered English	Regular Program with English for Speakers of Other Languages Support	TOTAL DISTRICT ENROLL MENT
Kindergarten	71	14	11	947
Grade 1	88	39	31	1102
Grade 2	93	42	20	985
Grade 3	78	21	25	968
Grade 4	64	23	28	1076
Grade 5	51	27	34	1005
Grade 6	27	37	35	1011
Grade 7	20	29	34	1084
Grade 8	22	16	28	966
Grade 9	0	0	60	956
Grade 10	0	0	25	957
Grade 11	0	0	8	894
Grade 12	0	0	5	733
TOTAL	514	248	344	12,684

SUMMARY:
- 4.1 % of the students in the School District are enrolled in the Primary Language Instruction phase
- 2.0% of the students in the School District are enrolled in the Sheltered English phase
- 2.7% of the students in the School District are enrolled in the Regular Program with English for Speakers of Other Languages phase

REVIEW OF LENGTH OF TIME IN THE BILINGUAL PROGRAM
FOR THE 1992–93 SIXTH GRADERS

To illustrate the length of time students stay in the bilingual program, the records of the 1992–93 sixth graders were reviewed. Data summarizing length of stay in various phases of the program is show, in the tables that follow. The data summarized on the following tables does not reflect the total number of students who have participated in the bilingual program in the last seven years since those who transferred out of the district prior to grade six are not reflected in these numbers.

As of October 1, 1992, there were 1011 grade six students in the participating School District. Of this number, 104 have been or are involved in some phase of the bilingual program. An additional twelve students have been involved in the program, but have not been in continuous attendance since date of entry and six other students are identified as special education students involved in the bilingual program. Shown on the attached tables is a summary of the movement of students through the bilingual program who have been in continuous attendance. This summary excludes the bilingual education students and those who have not been in continuous attendance.

The tables present the information based on the grade upon entry. In other words, the following question was asked: What happened to present grade six students who have been or are part of the bilingual program, categorized by the grade at entry?

The information below is provided as an explanation for how to read tables A through G. Each table represents current sixth graders, but in addition, each table represents a different entry level grade. For example, all of table A represents current sixth graders who started in some phase of the bilingual program at the kindergarten level.

EXAMPLE:

Look at the first horizontal line of numbers on table A. It should be read as follows:

> Two of the present grade six students entered the School District as kindergarten students. They spent one year in primary language instruction, five years in sheltered English, and are presently in the regular program receiving support in English for Speakers of Other Languages (ESOL).

The last horizontal line of table A should be read as follows:

> Two of the present grade six students entered the program at the ESOL phase. They remained there for one year, and then spent six years in the regular program, including this year.

The information in tables A–G can also be summarized to show where the sixth graders are at this time based upon grade at entry.

22 of the present sixth graders entered some phase of the bilingual program in kindergarten.

> 0 are in Primary Language Instruction
> 4 are in Sheltered English
> 12 are in Regular Program with ESOL Support
> 6 are in Regular Program

21 of the present sixth graders entered some phase of the bilingual program in first grade.

> 1 is in Primary Language Instruction
> 4 are in Sheltered English
> 6 are in Regular Program with ESOL Support
> 10 are in Regular Program

19 of the present sixth graders entered some phase of the bilingual program in second grade.

> 2 are in Primary Language Instruction
> 5 are in Sheltered English
> 4 are in Regular Program with ESOL Support
> 8 are in Regular Program

18 of the present sixth graders entered some phase of the bilingual program in third grade.

> 4 are in Primary Language Instruction
> 4 are in Sheltered English
> 1 is in Regular Program with ESOL Support
> 9 are in Regular Program

6 of the present sixth graders entered some phase of the bilingual program in fourth grade.

> 2 are in Primary Language Instruction
> 1 is in Sheltered English
> 1 is in Regular Program with ESOL Support
> 2 are in Regular Program

11 of the present sixth graders entered some phase of the bilingual program in fifth grade.

> 8 are in Primary Language Instruction
> 1 is in Sheltered English
> 1 is in Regular Program with ESOL Support
> 1 is in Regular Program

7 of the present sixth graders entered some phase of the bilingual program in sixth grade.

> 5 are in Primary Language Instruction
> 2 are in Regular Program with ESOL Support

PROGRAM HISTORY FOR PRESENT GRADE 6 STUDENTS WITH NO INTERRUPTIONS IN ATTENDANCE SINCE DATE OF ENTRY WHO WERE/ARE IN THE BILINGUAL PROGRAM

TABLE A: STUDENTS WHO ENTERED IN KINDERGARTEN

NUMBER OF YEARS in Each Program Phase

Number of Students	Primary Language Instruction	Sheltered English	Regular Program with ESOL Support	Regular Program
2	1	5	1	
1	2	4	1	
1	2	5		
1	2		2	3
2	4	2	1	
1	4	3		
1		8		
1		7		
1		2	2	3
1		5	1	1
7		6	1	
1		2	3	2
2			1	6

Total Number of Students who Entered at Primary Language Phase = 8
Total Number of Students who Entered at Sheltered English Phase = 12
Total Number of Students who Entered at Regular Program with ESOL Phase = 2
Total Number of Students = 22

**PROGRAM HISTORY FOR PRESENT GRADE 6 STUDENTS WITH
NO INTERRUPTIONS IN ATTENDANCE
SINCE DATE OF ENTRY
WHO WERE/ARE IN THE BILINGUAL PROGRAM**

TABLE B: STUDENTS WHO ENTERED IN GRADE 1

NUMBER OF YEARS in Each Program Phase

Number of Students	Primary Language Instruction	Sheltered English	Regular Program with ESOL Support	Regular Program
1	6			
2	5	1		
1	4	2		
1	4	1	1	
1	3	3		
1	2	3	1	
1	2	2	2	
1*	1	1	3	1
1		6	1	
1		5	1	
1		1	4	1
1			6	
3			5	1
1			3	3
4			1	5

Total Number of Students who Entered at Primary Language Phase = 9
Total Number of Students who Entered at Sheltered English Phase = 3
Total Number of Students who Entered at Regular Program with ESOL Phase = 9
Total Number of Students = 21
*Waiver

**PROGRAM HISTORY FOR PRESENT GRADE 6 STUDENTS WITH
NO INTERRUPTIONS IN ATTENDANCE
SINCE DATE OF ENTRY
WHO WERE/ARE IN THE BILINGUAL PROGRAM**

TABLE C: STUDENTS WHO ENTERED IN GRADE 2

NUMBER OF YEARS in Each Program Phase

Number of Students	Primary Language Instruction	Sheltered English	Regular Program with ESOL Support	Regular Program
2	5			
1	4	2		
2	4	1		
2	3	2		
1	2	1	1	1
1	2	2	1	
1	1	2	1	1
1	1	1	2	1
2		2	1	
1		3	1	1
1			2	3
1			3	2
1			4	1
1			5	

Total Number of Students who Entered at Primary Language Phase = 11
Total Number of Students who Entered at Sheltered English Phase = 3
Total Number of Students who Entered at Regular Program with ESOL Phase = 5
Total Number of Students = 19

PROGRAM HISTORY FOR PRESENT GRADE 6 STUDENTS WITH
NO INTERRUPTIONS IN ATTENDANCE
SINCE DATE OF ENTRY
WHO WERE/ARE IN THE BILINGUAL PROGRAM

TABLE D: STUDENTS WHO ENTERED IN GRADE 3

NUMBER OF YEARS in Each Program Phase

Number of Students	Primary Language Instruction	Sheltered English	Regular Program with ESOL Support	Regular Program
4	4			
1	3	1		
1	2	2		
1	1	3		
1		4		
1		2	1	1
2		1	2	1
1		1	1	2
1			5	
2			3	1
1			2	3
2				3

Total Number of Students who Entered at Primary Language Phase = 7
Total Number of Students who Entered at Sheltered English Phase = 5
Total Number of Students who Entered at Regular Program with ESOL Phase = 6
Total Number of Students = 18

PROGRAM HISTORY FOR PRESENT GRADE 6 STUDENTS WITH NO INTERRUPTIONS IN ATTENDANCE SINCE DATE OF ENTRY WHO WERE/ARE IN THE BILINGUAL PROGRAM

TABLE E: STUDENTS WHO ENTERED IN GRADE 4

NUMBER OF YEARS in Each Program Phase

Number of Students	Primary Language Instruction	Sheltered English	Regular Program with ESOL Support	Regular Program
2	3			
1	1	2		
1		1	1	1
1			3	
1			2	1

Total Number of Students who Entered at Primary Language Phase = 3
Total Number of Students who Entered at Sheltered English Phase = 1
Total Number of Students who Entered at Regular Program with ESOL Phase =2
Total Number of Students = 6

**PROGRAM HISTORY FOR PRESENT GRADE 6 STUDENTS WITH
NO INTERRUPTIONS IN ATTENDANCE
SINCE DATE OF ENTRY
WHO WERE/ARE IN THE BILINGUAL PROGRAM**

TABLE F: STUDENTS WHO ENTERED IN GRADE 5

NUMBER OF YEARS in Each Program Phase

Number of Students	Primary Language Instruction	Sheltered English	Regular Program with ESOL Support	Regular Program
8	2			
1		2		
1		1	1	
1			1	1

Total Number of Students who Entered at Primary Language Phase = 8
Total Number of Students who Entered at Sheltered English Phase = 2
Total Number of Students who Entered at Regular Program with ESOL Phase = 1
Total Number of Students = 11

PROGRAM HISTORY FOR PRESENT GRADE 6 STUDENTS WITH NO INTERRUPTIONS IN ATTENDANCE SINCE DATE OF ENTRY WHO WERE/ARE IN THE BILINGUAL PROGRAM

TABLE G: STUDENTS WHO ENTERED IN GRADE 6

NUMBER OF YEARS in Each Program Phase

Number of Students	Primary Language Instruction	Sheltered English	Regular Program with ESOL Support	Regular Program
5	1			
2			1	

Total Number of Students who Entered at Primary Language Phase = 5
Total Number of Students who Entered at Sheltered English Phase = 0
Total Number of Students who Entered at Regular Program with ESOL Phase = 2
Total Number of Students = 7

TABLE H: SUMMARY OF THE PROGRAM PHASE ENTERED BY
PRESENT GRADE 6 STUDENTS WHO HAVE HAD
NO INTERRUPTIONS IN ATTENDANCE SINCE
DATE OF ENTRY

Grade	Number who Entered at Primary Language Instruction Phase	Number who Entered at Sheltered English Phase	Number who Entered at Regular Program with ESOL Support Phase	Total Number of Students
Kindergarten	8	12	2	22
Grade 1	9	3	9	21
Grade 2	11	3	5	19
Grade 3	7	5	6	18
Grade 4	3	1	2	6
Grade 5	8	2	1	11
Grade 6	5		2	7
TOTAL	51	25	27	104

TABLE I: SUMMARY OF THE NUMBER OF GRADE 6 STUDENTS
WHO HAVE HAD NO INTERRUPTIONS IN ATTENDANCE
WHO ARE IN REGULAR PROGRAM OR REGULAR PROGRAM
WITH ESOL SUPPORT IN GRADE 6

Grades	Number of 6th Grade Students Who Entered the Bilingual Program at Each Grade Level	Number of Students Who have Exited to Regular Program with or without ESOL Support
Kindergarten	22	18
Grade 1	21	16
Grade 2	19	12
Grade 3	18	10
Grade 4	6	3
Grade 5	11	2
Grade 6	7	2
TOTAL	104	63

BIBLIOGRAPHY

Bamford, K. & Nizokawa, D. *Cognitive Development of Children in an Additive-Bilingual Program: The Third Report.* Paper. Annual Meeting of the American Educational Research Association. Boston, MA, April 1990.

Bilingual Education. Phi Delta Kappa. Bloomington, Ind., 1988.

Bilingual Education Handbook. California Department of Education. Sacramento, Cal., 1990.

Bilingual Education: Time to Take a Second Look? Phi Delta Kappa. Bloomington, Ind., 1990.

Chamot, Anna. *A Transfer Curriculum for Teaching Content Based ESL in the Elementary School.* Paper. Annual Convention of Teachers of English to Speakers of Other Languages. Toronto, Canada, March 1983.

Crawford, James. Bilingual Education: Language, Learning, and Politics. *Education Week,* April 1, 1987, 19–50.

Cummins, Jim. *Empowering Minority Students.* California Association for Bilingual Education. Sacramento, Cal., 1989.

Fuhriman, J. *When They Don't Speak English. How Do We Educate?* Paper. Annual Convention of the National School Boards Association. San Francisco, Cal., April 1983.

Guidelines for Educational Programs in the Commonwealth of Pennsylvania for Limited English Proficient Children. Pennsylvania Department of Education, 1986.

Landry, M. *Improving English Language Competency Among ESL Second Grade Children Through a Socially Interactive Communicative Language Teaching (CLT Program).* Dissertation. Nova University, 1990.

Lessow-Hurley, Judith A. *A Commonsense Guide to Bilingual Education.* Association for Curriculum and Development. Alexandria, Va., 1991.

National Academy of Sciences Validates Importance of Native Language Instruction. *NABE News.* National Association for Bilingual Education. July 1, 1992, XV, 7.

New York City Staff Development Program for Bilingual Early Childhood Teachers 1984–1985. New York City Board of Education, Office of Educational Assessment, 1986.

Prabhu, N. There Is No Best Method–Why? *TESOL Quarterly,* Summer 1990, 24, 16, 176.

Ramirez, J. David & others. *Longitudinal Study of Structured English Immersion Strategy. Early Exit and Late-Exit Transitional Bilingual Education Programs for Language-Minority Children.* U.S. Department of Education. Washington, D.C., February 1991.

Reyher, J. & Garcia, R. Helping Minorities Read Better: Problems and Promises. *Reading Research and Instruction,* 1989, 28, 854–91.

Rhodes, N. & Richardson, G. *Total and Partial Immersion Programs in U.S. Elementary Schools. 1989: and Useful Resources for Teaching Languages to Children.* Center for Applied Linguistics. Washington, D.C., 1989.

Second Language Learning by Young Children. Child Development Programs Advisory Committee, Sacramento, Cal., 1985.

Soto, Lourdes. *Teacher Preparation and the Linguistically Diverse Young Child.* The Pennsylvania State University, University Park, Pa., 1991.

Valencia, Atilano. *A Comparative and Descriptive Review of Four Types of Bilingual Education Paradigms.* New Mexico State University, Las Cruces, N.M., 1981.

Yap, K. & others. *Making a Difference for the Bilingual Child: How One District Achieved its Goals.* Paper. Annual Meeting of the American Educational Research Association. Boston, Mass., April 1990.

APPENDIX B

The Superintendent's Response
to the Bilingual Committee

- I know this is a controversial issue with many different opinions on how to best teach L.E.P. children English.
- My strongest objection to the current program as well as the recommendations in the report preserved is the length of time Latino L.E.P. students spend in the bilingual program.
- The report issued by the committee does not address learning needs of non-Latino L.E.P.'s in the same manner as Latino L.E.P.'s.
- Further, I have concerns about emphasis that is being placed on the Latino culture through the term of this program. There is no other program in the school as an emphasis of maintaining any one ethnic group's culture as part of classroom instruction. An appreciation of all cultures is taught through our World Cultures and Foreign Language Programs.
- I have a concern about the transition of a student in our bilingual education program in eighth grade who will be moving into the high school.
- By delaying early English acquisition, we deny some minority students equal opportunities in the high school program of studies.
- But, when you boil it down, there are really only three main options in teaching non-English speaking children to speak English in traditional bilingual education, which is [blank] current program, structured immersion, and ESL.
- The research is mixed—let me repeat—the research is mixed. There is no right way that is conclusively and exclusively supported by the research. It comes down to what each school district and community is comfortable with. I believe the decision to use one approach or the other is an educational one. It should not be a political, cultural, social, or even economic one.

THE COMMITTEE, WHO PUT TOGETHER THE REPORT AND RECOMMENDA-TIONS, DID SO BASED ON THEIR BELIEF SYSTEM WHICH I GUESS, ABSENT CLEAR AND UNCHALLENGED RESEARCH, IS A VIABLE WAY TO APPROACH THIS QUESTION. THE COMMITTEE IS SAYING THAT THEY UNANIMOUSLY BELIEVE:

1. We believe the present program design is based upon accepted research. I agree with that, but I remind you again that there is another school of thought out

there, supported by accepted research that gives great credence to structured immersion as the best way to go. I believe our bilingual education program should contain only two components:

Option #1: English as a Second Language

English as a second language (ESL) is a program for LEP students that is particularly designed to teach English to non-English speakers through the use of audiovisual materials. ESL teachers do not use the home language of LEP students in these programs.

LEP students progress from basic ESL through intermediate ESL to advanced ESL usually in less than one and one-half years. They then attend regular classes in their local schools. During the time that LEP students are enrolled in the ESL program, they may spend half their school day in regular classes that do not require much ability to speak English in order to succeed in those classes, e[blank], shop, or physical education.

Option #2: Structured Immersion

Immersion is an instructional program in which teachers only speak English to LEP students. The teacher in an immersion program, however, understands the language of LEP students, and the students may speak to the teacher in the language spoken at home. If the teacher occasionally "cues" LEP students in the home language for purposes of clarification, then this instructional approach is known as *structured* immersion. LEP students learn English and subject content at the same time through a curriculum that introduces subject matter based upon the assumption that the learners have no prior knowledge of English, i.e., the introduction of new vocabulary words is carefully controlled.

While the great preponderance of local programs serving LEP students have been of the "bilingual education" nature, providing subject matter instruction in the home language of the LEP students, there is some limited research on the effectiveness of several immersion projects in the United States.

Baker and de Kanter reported on an evaluation of an English immersion program for Mexican-American students in McAllen, Texas; the LEP students in the study were from low-income families who had minimal involvement in their children's school program. Over a 9-month period, the 78 LEP students that were randomly assigned to the English immersion program made significant gains in both English and Spanish proficiency over 78 LEP students that were randomly assigned to the bilingual education program.

More recently, Russell Gersten, in an article entitled, "Structured Immersion for Language Minority Students: Results of a Longitudinal Evaluation," reported on an evaluation of a *structured* immersion program that has been operating for the past seven years at a school on the West Coast. The LEP students involved are Asian or from the Pacific Islands, almost all of whom are from low-income families. The program, which was initiated in 1979, combines developmental and remedial instruction in an ungraded model for LEP students of kindergarten through sixth grade age. Rather than isolate the LEP students by placing them in a separate classroom, the program integrates them with English-speaking students working at many skills levels. All academic instruction is in English at a level understood by the LEP students. In addition, there are always bilingual instructors in the class who understand the LEP students' home language and translate problematic words or answer questions in the home language. Further, the curriculum is structured to carefully control the vocabulary and sequence of the lessons so that prior knowledge of English is not assumed or required.

In the intermediate grades (third through sixth), the researchers assessed all LEP students who were in the structured immersion program for at least eight full months. They found significant improvement in reading, math, and English proficiency in two successive samples of LEP students, the 1980–81 group and the 1981–82 group. The fact that these academic gains were replicated with two successive groups of LEP students is used by the researchers to support the ideas that the gains were due to the structured immersion program, as opposed to the particular group of LEP students participating in the study.

At the primary level (first and second grades), the researchers measured the LEP students' academic performance in the structured immersion program in comparison to the performance of a comparable group of LEP students enrolled in the school district's bilingual education program. The results revealed substantial differences in reading and math achievement, but not in English-language proficiency. Seventy-five percent of the LEP students in the structured immersion program were at or above grade level in reading, and 96 percent were at or above grade level in math. By contrast, of the LEP students in the bilingual education program, only 19 percent were at or above grade level in reading; 62 percent were above grade level in math.

These results, according to Gersten, would seem to indicate that the structured immersion program was an effective approach for acquisition of reading and math skills and proficiency in written English for low-income Asian students entering school with limited English proficiency. There also appears to be evidence that the program's effects were maintained up to two years after the LEP students completed the program.

3. We believe that all students should become proficient in English.

I agree, but should we take five to seven years to accomplish this important goal? Quite simply stated, I have concerns about the length of time our present program is taking to have Latino students acquire adequate skills in reading, writing, and speaking English. L.E.P. students of other languages accelerate much faster into regular education than their Latino counterparts mainly due to the fact that the only option available to them is E.S.O.L. The structured immersion approach is much faster, and according to the research, does the job of having non-English speakers learn the English language so they can be competitive with their Anglo counterparts in regular education, higher education, and in the job market.

Latino students, as well as all other language speaking students, need to be prepared in English as soon as possible so they are better prepared to elect regular education courses offered at the middle school, and especially, the high school levels. Just like their Anglo counterparts.

5. We believe that having a strong foundation in the native language promotes a smooth transition to learning in English.

I strongly disagree, and the research does not exclusively support this contention. I have problems accepting keeping a five-year old kindergarten child who comes to school only speaking Spanish in a Spanish only program through K–1–2 and yes possibly third grade before ever concentrating on learning English. We all know that the younger a child is the easier it is to teach a new language. If it's true, you can't teach an old dog new tricks, I wonder if the converse is also true—I believe it is.

7. We believe there are two levels of language proficiency: conversational and academic. Generally it takes one to three years to achieve conversational proficiency and an additional three to four years to achieve academic proficiency.

I disagree—and many immigrants who come to this country speaking no English would also disagree—and again may I say that the research does not exclusively support this contention.

8. We believe that a student will be no more proficient in his second language than he is in his first language.

I disagree—Are you saying that a kindergarten child who speaks fluent Spanish cannot learn to speak fluent English until he/she is able to read in Spanish first[blank]?

10. We believe children build on prior knowledge developed in their native language; therefore, teaching children in their native language helps to build background knowledge, which will empower them to succeed in school.

I strongly disagree with this statement.

11. We believe that educating the child in the native language promotes positive self-esteem, enhances critical thinking, and helps prepare the child for participation in society.

    I disagree—I believe that whenever we give children the prerequisite skills for success, we enhance self-esteem. The sooner we can have children competitive, the sooner we can ensure success and thereby promote positive experiences that will automatically promote and enhance their self-esteem and self-image.

12. We believe that one maximizes the potential for parental involvement when the language of instruction matches the home language.

    I probably agree—but aren't we having children pay a terrible price for the possibility of maximizing the potential for parental involvement? Then when should the transition ever occur? And aren't there better ways to address this important need?

13. We believe that native language instruction accelerates growth in areas such as reading, mathematics, and English language for second language learners as compared to limited English proficient students who have not used native language instruction.

    I disagree—quite frankly, there is too much evidence to the contrary. L.E.P. students in languages other than Spanish are making it in our schools, as well as schools across the country in E.S.O.L. support programs. With the numbers of L.E.P. Latino children in Steel Town, I believe a combination of structured immersion and E.S.O.L. would be a fine combination to accomplish the goals of English proficiency in the least amount of time.

14. We believe that the middle school program should be a transitional period between the elementary and high school programs.

    I agree that the last chance we have to aggressively pursue the goal of English proficiency is in our middle schools.
    The high school is too late and we should only have students in a high school bilingual program who entered our school district as high school-aged students with little or no English proficiency. The current program allows for students who were in our middle school bilingual program, and in many instances, our elementary bilingual program to continue in high school E.S.O.L. programs. And may I stress that this, less than aggressive approach, prevents

those Latino students from participating in all of the courses available to their Anglo counterparts and thereby does not afford them equal academic and/or vocational education opportunities. It also hampers social interaction by denying them regular programs and activities. (One room schoolhouse.)

IN ADDITION TO MY CONCERNS REGARDING (1) THE LENGTH OF TIME A STUDENT SPENDS IN THE BILINGUAL PROGRAM, (2) THE EMPHASIS ON THE MAINTENANCE OF THE LATINO CULTURE, AND (3) THE EFFECTS DELAYED ENGLISH ACQUISITION HAS ON AFFORDING LATINO MINORITY STUDENTS EQUAL OPPORTUNITY IN THE PROGRAM OF STUDIES, I ALSO WOULD LIKE TO ADDRESS:

Recommendation 6: Class Size

We need to further review the rationale for maintaining 18:1 class sizes in our primary language, Spanish only classes. I'm not sure we have stand alone justification for 18:1 in these classes when compared to other classes in the district.

Recommendation 9: Program Evaluation

You need to know that I have previously denied this request. My reasoning for the denial was because, and I have told this to the committee, I am not calling into question whether the educational bilingual program being used in the BASD works or not. The central question is should we keep a child in the transitional bilingual education program for an average of five to seven years to accomplish our desired results. An outside evaluation of our current program will not answer that question. That is the central issue and the main concern I have—not whether what we are doing is working but is there a better way to achieve the desired results.

AS I HAVE SAID IN MY OPENING REMARKS, I RESPECT THE COMMITTEE'S VIEWPOINT. HOWEVER, AS SUPERINTENDENT OF SCHOOLS, I FEEL IT IS MY RESPONSIBILITY TO ASSURE ALL STUDENTS AN EQUAL EDUCATION AND THE OPPORTUNITY TO BE THE BEST THEY CAN BE. I FEEL THAT THE CONTINUATION OF THE PRESENT BILINGUAL EDUCATION PROGRAM CAN ONLY HINDER THE EDUCATIONAL PROGRESS OF THESE STUDENTS. I STRONGLY BELIEVE THAT THE EARLIEST ACQUISITION OF ENGLISH LANGUAGE SKILLS SHOULD AND MUST BE THE MAIN OBJECTIVE OF THE PROGRAM.

BILINGUAL EDUCATION PROGRAM
POSSIBLE COURSES OF ACTION

OPTION #1:   Accept the recommendations of the Bilingual Education Committee as submitted and/or with modifications.

OPTION #2:   Direct that a program be developed to incorporate the philosophical perspective offered by the superintendent.

OPTION #3:   Approve a pilot structured immersion program to evaluate the benefits compared to the current transitional bilingual program.

OPTION #4:   Hire a consulting firm to review the committee's recommendations, the philosophical perspective offered by the superintendent of schools and the type of program that would result from it, and other viable options which meet the needs of limited English proficient students in the Steel Town School District.

At the conclusion of the study, the consultants should recommend a program design for each level of the system which best meets the needs of all limited English proficient students in our school district.

APPENDIX C

Report from the English Acquisition Committee:
A Ticket for Tomorrow

INTRODUCTION

In February, 1993, thirty of the School District educators came together to begin the process of designing a new program for limited English proficient students based on the goal and objectives approved by the Board of School Directors at its meeting on February 1. The goal and objectives are as follows:

Goal: The goal of the English Acquisition program is to have all limited English proficient (L.E.P.) students become fluent in English in the shortest amount of time so they may experience maximum success in school.

Objective 1—To the extent possible, provide for limited English proficient (L.E.P.) students in their home schools.

Objective 2—To develop a program of English language acquisition for L.E.P. students of all nationalities which will achieve the goal of English proficiency in a maximum of three years.

Objective 3—To provide special ongoing programs for parents of L.E.P. students to make them aware of the school's goal and solicit their support.

Objective 4—To provide specialized tutorial and guidance services including a home/school communication component at the middle school and elementary level to ensure that L.E.P. students achieve their maximum potential with respect to academic and vocational pursuits.

Objective 5—To provide specialized tutorial, guidance, and placement services including a home/school communication component at the home school level to ensure that the academic achievement of L.E.P. students is at a level that will enable them to select business, vocational/technical, or college preparatory programs of studies, and upon graduation, be able to enter the work force or pursue further education fully prepared to be successful.

Objective 6—To provide each high school L.E.P. student with an adult and/or student mentor for additional support to assist in adjusting to high school life, selecting a program of studies, and exploring various career options.

Objective 7—To assess the current World Cultures Program and other appropriate curricular areas, K–12, to determine whether the curriculum reflects a multicultural approach and, if required, to make modifications.

Objective 8—To develop programs that foster positive relationships among students and staff in which respect for others is a foremost goal.

This interim report is designed to address primarily Objectives 1 and 2. Although Objectives 3–8 have been discussed, and portions of them are included in the sections that follow, the primary focus of the report remains a description of the English language acquisition program recommended for the three levels of our system for implementation for the 1993–94 school year. The principal of the Elementary School presented information to the board in January, 1993, which highlighted successful English immersion programs in the country. One of those programs was from a retired director of the ESL Program, who met with the English Acquisition Design Team during its first meeting to present information and brainstorm ideas. During the months that followed, members of the team visited several schools and the neighboring school district. Team members had the opportunity to interact extensively with principals and teachers about the programs. From this early beginning, team members began to frame a program that would meet the needs of students, taking ideas that would work, and rejecting those not appropriate.

Some of the work of the team was done as a committee of the whole, but much of the design for each level of our system was carried out by subcommittees of the overall team who work at that level. The committee as a whole decided to categorize LEP students into three levels: beginner, intermediate, or advanced, based on their proficiency in reading, writing, speaking and listening. Final descriptions for each of these levels are being completed. A fourth category, known as low schooled, was developed for a select group of secondary students who share some or all of the following characteristics:

Beginning learner
Did not attend school on a regular basis—sparse attendance
Atypical discrepancy between age and grade placement
Underdeveloped math concepts
Unable to communicate coherently in the first or second language
Lacks knowledge of school social norms.

A Center for Language Assessment (CLA) will assess students and provide information to schools to assist in placing of students. Evaluation tests have been selected and training is planned on their use. Contrary to the present system, the Center for Language Assessment (CLA) will not play a major role in moving students from one level to another or exiting them from the program. The design team believes this decision is best left to the building level professionals who work with each student. Data will be collected periodically by the CLA to monitor and track the progress of students in the program. This information will be used in the future to determine the effectiveness of the overall English acquisition program.

Members of the design team met with administrators and teachers involved in the present bilingual special education classes to review the impact of the proposed changes.

The team has estimated the number of students who will need service as LEP students next year as follows:

SCHOOL	NUMBER OF L.E.P. STUDENTS	PERCENT OF TOTAL POPULATION
	6	<1
	8	3
	6	2
	48	12
	225	46
	4	1
	33	6
		25
	100	
	13	3
	1	<1
	81	23
	129	39
	4	2
	4	1
	11	3
	11	4
	112	19
	121	<1
	16	2
	64	8
	20	6

Based on the numbers above, programs for each level of our system are presented below.

ELEMENTARY SCHOOL MODEL

GENERAL INFORMATION

Language learning is most effective when it is a means of communicating meaningful information. ESL researchers recommend organizing language instruction around the content area subjects and providing thematically integrated units of learning. This will help students to learn content-related information while acquiring English skills in listening, speaking, reading, and writing.

The overall goal of the elementary school model is to integrate LEP students into heterogeneous classes, to use literature-based reading and writing instruction and oral language to accelerate learning for all students, and to coordinate the child's educational program to reduce fragmentation. Because of a large disparity among the schools in the number of LEP students who need service, schools were placed in the following broad categories:

HIGH IMPACT:

MEDIUM IMPACT:

LOW IMPACT:

The LEP students in the high and medium impact schools, with some exceptions, will receive their program in their home school. Since there is lack of space to accommodate all of the LEP students who reside within its boundaries, it is proposed to move the students who are identified as Primary Language students this year. Students in the low impact schools may be grouped in low impact centers, or receive the program in their home school. This decision will be made on a case by case and school by school basis, depending upon the number of students who need service, the availability of resources in the building to meet the student's needs, and the age of the student.

PROGRAM DESCRIPTION

HIGH IMPACT SCHOOLS

The program for the high impact schools, at the Elementary School, was created with the following philosophy in mind:

- To provide an academic setting that accelerates the acquisition of English
- To integrate LEP students into ALL classes
- To increase all students' oral language proficiency
- To develop learners who can apply knowledge to the acquisition of knowledge
- To create an educational setting that will enhance the acquisition of basic reading, writing and mathematical skills
- To integrate the Instructional Support concepts of collaboration, adaptation, and Curriculum Based Assessment into the school program
- To coordinate the child's educational program to reduce fragmentation
- To integrate whole language philosophy into the classroom
- To provide native language support for concept clarification where possible

To provide a program that meets the above philosophy, the team believes it is imperative that the usual pupil-to-teacher ratio be reduced. Since LEP students will be integrated into all classes, this means, for example, that approximately half of each class will have special language needs. The team believes these needs can not be met with 26–28 students in a classroom. Therefore, all classrooms have been restaffed at a ratio of approximately 18/20-to-1. The present program for LEP students at the elementary level separates the LEP students from their English speaking peers for much of the school day. This proposal keeps LEP students and their English speaking peers *together* for most of each day. Students categorized as beginner level LEP students will receive ESOL instruction as a pull-out for approximately 75 minutes each day. While the ESOL students are out of the room, the classroom teacher has the opportunity to intensify instruction with the remaining students. It is essential that a flexible schedule be developed to address the needs of the LEP student, while at the same time reducing the number of pullouts in a child's schedule. An important feature of this plan is to limit the number of teachers who provide basic instruction for each child.

MEDIUM IMPACT SCHOOLS

The program for medium impact schools shares the same philosophy as described above for high impact schools: LEP students are integrated into heterogeneous classes in their home school, using the literature-based reading and writing instruction and oral language development to accelerate learning for all students. LEP students will receive approximately 75 minutes daily of ESOL instruction. This instruction may be a pull-out or a push-in approach. Class size for the medium impact schools may be reduced, dependent upon the number of LEP students, particularly beginners, anticipated for each class. If there are few beginners, the ratios have remained between 25–28 students and those with a larger number of beginners are staffed between 20–24 students per class.

Low Impact Schools

The low-impact schools are so designated because there are very few students in each school who need ESOL services. These schools will be served by either an itinerant ESOL teacher if three or more students need service or by the reading specialist, a special tutor, or some other appropriate instructor if only one or two students need service. If the number of students who need ESOL service at a school is only one or two, the design team believes it may be necessary to place the beginner level student in a nearby school where ESOL is offered until the student has acquired "survival" English. LEP students at the intermediate and advanced levels will remain in their home schools. Kindergarten and first graders, regardless of language level, remain in their home schools. The design team is in the process of gathering information on each student in these schools and will review with the building administrator and present ESOL teacher the level of service needed for each student. A plan will then be finalized for how best to deliver the ESOL services when this is concluded.

MIDDLE SCHOOL MODEL

General Information

The English Acquisition Program, Middle School Model, incorporates the teaching concept of the middle school philosophy as its cornerstone. Most Limited English Proficient (LEP) students will be assigned to a traditional academic team at an appropriate grade level for all their academic instruction. Secondly, this model returns most LEP students to their home schools.

The Middle School Model is divided into four phases: the beginning learner (low-schooled), the beginner, the intermediate and the advanced. The first two phases will be housed at one middle school center, while the last two phases will be, for the most part, delivered at the student's home school. Students considered to be in the beginner, intermediate or advanced levels will be grouped within an academic team. While the beginning learner level will be structured as a self-contained program, it is expected that a typical learner will spend three years in the program, if they enter at the beginner level, and less, if they enter as an intermediate or advanced level student. Beginning learners may need more than three years in the program to attain an appropriate level of English competency.

There are several general understandings which have been proposed as a part of the middle school model. The first is the important role the Advisor (homeroom teacher) will play in the life of the LEP student. All LEP students will be assigned to an Advisor/Advisee group in the appropriate grade level and team. The Advisors will be responsible for assigning a "buddy" to each LEP student in his/her group, fostering the buddy relationship, rewarding the buddy in some way perhaps with an "A" in citizenship, recognizing the efforts of the buddy publicly at an awards assembly, and monitoring progress in functional English word/phrases acquisition. It is expected that all LEP students will be able to use "survival" English words and phrases as soon as possible, so that they may access the services of the lavatory, cafeteria, classroom, office, nurse, water fountain, and, in addition, personal identification information and teacher and principal names. To complement this advisor/advisee buddy program, each school will offer an activity during their Activity Period to train the "buddies" and to plan special activities for the LEP students.

It is also very important to provide LEP students with an extended opportunity for learning. Each middle school will, therefore, offer a formal tutoring period from 3:00–3:45 PM at the end of each school day. Staffed by the ESOL teacher, this program will offer students opportunities for peer tutoring, mentor tutoring, homework club and an after-school center, where students can receive the extra support they need during their acquisition of the English language and also after they have been completely mainstreamed into the regular program.

In addition, this model requires initial and on-going staff development opportunities for both the ESOL staff and the regular education staff, such as, knowledge of the English acquisition program, ESOL techniques to be used with the LEP students to encourage speaking and writing, learning styles research, cooperative learning techniques, multicultural sensitivity training, alternate assessment strategies, and the use of technology.

The middle school model also requires that the assignment of staff remain flexible both within the district and within the school. The reassignment of staff at any time to meet student enrollment needs must be supported.

And, lastly, students will be moved through the ESOL levels as a result of an articulated assessment model implemented by a school-based decision making team including the ESOL teacher, regular academic and/or guidance personnel and administration.

PROGRAM DESCRIPTION

BEGINNING LEARNER (LOW-SCHOOLED)

The Beginning learner phase is designed for the twelve to fifteen students across all four middle schools who have received a limited or interrupted education prior to their enrollment in our district. These students usually exhibit severe deficits in basic skills in their native language and also require the development of social skills and appropriate school behavior. Since their needs are many, this program phase will be delivered at a center, probably at the Middle School, in a self-contained classroom setting, staffed by an ESOL teacher and a teacher aide. This was chosen because it also houses the middle school alternative education program. After one year at the beginning learner phase, each student's progress will be evaluated to determine whether they are able to move into the regular ESOL program, either at the beginner or intermediate level, or whether they are candidates for the alternative education program.

The academic program will consist of three periods of ESOL instruction, one period of individualized mathematics instruction delivered with technology and one period of science/social studies concepts. Modification in programming will be determined by the needs of the students. This instructional program will be delivered in a self-contained classroom structure by an ESOL teacher and a teacher aide. Beginning learners may be assigned to advisor/advisee, activity period offerings and two periods of related arts, when the teacher determines the student has internalized the school behavioral norms. Students will interact with native English speakers during advisor/advisee, lunch, related arts and activity period.

In addition to the instructional program, these students will be involved in a formal proactive guidance/counseling program delivered by the guidance counselor. The classroom teacher will also deliver a self-esteem building program as an integral part of this program.

BEGINNER

The program for students at the beginner level will be delivered in a middle school center to be determined. This beginner ESOL group will be part of a trained, sensitized, inserviced academic teacher team at the appropriate grade level to be determined by each school.

The academic program will consist of three periods of ESOL instruction delivered by the ESOL teacher, one period of mathematics delivered by the regular math teacher and one period of Science/Social Studies concepts course, delivered by the regular science and social studies teachers for a semester each. The team with the ESOL class will be started with an additional academic teacher, who will join the mathematics, science and social studies classes, while the regular reading and language arts teachers will pull into the ESOL classes, thereby assigning two full-time teachers to each beginner class. All beginner students will be assigned to team advisor/advisee groups and two periods of related arts with their buddies. Students will interact with native English speakers during advisor/advisee, lunch, related arts and activity period.

INTERMEDIATE

The program for intermediate level students will be delivered in the home school. The academic program will consist of two periods of ESOL as a pull-out from Language Arts (grades 6, 7, 8) and from reading in grade 6, reading and philosophy in grade 7 and health and typing in grade 8. Students will be assigned to a regular academic section(s) in their appropriate grade level and will receive instruction in the regular mathematics, science and social studies classes from the regular academic teachers. To eliminate the risk to LEP students, the grading in science and social studies will be A/S/N rather than the traditional system of A/B/C/D/F.

In low-intensity schools, ESOL students may be assigned to one team at each grade level; in high-intensity schools, ESOL students may be assigned to as many teams as necessary to ensure an adequate ratio between LEP students and native English speakers. ESOL classes may be multi-graded and multi-leveled in low intensity schools, while in high-intensity schools, regrouping of students by language acquisition level and/or grade level may be possible.

These students will also be assigned to a team advisor/advisee group and related arts with their buddies. During the remedial reading class in the related arts band, ESOL students will receive support, tailored to their individual needs in the regular courses from the reading staff or other available "as assigned" staff.

Students at the intermediate level will interact with native English speakers for homeroom, lunch, activity period, related arts, mathematics, science and social studies.

ADVANCED

The program for advanced level students will be delivered in the home school. The academic program will consist of one period of ESOL as a pull-out from reading in grade 6, reading and philosophy in grade 7 and health and typing in grade 8. Students will be assigned to a regular academic section(s) in their appropriate grade level and will receive instruction in the regular language arts, mathematics, science and social studies classes from the regular academic teachers. The evaluation in science and social studies may be A/S/N or the regular grading system, which will be determined cooperatively by the ESOL teacher, the academic teacher involved and the student.

In low-intensity schools, ESOL students may be assigned to one team at each grade level; in high-intensity schools, ESOL students may be assigned to as many teams as necessary to ensure an adequate ratio between LEP students and native English speakers. ESOL classes may be multi-graded and multi-leveled in low-intensity schools, while in high-intensity schools, regrouping of students by language acquisition level and/or grade level may be possible. ESOL and regular language arts teachers will coordinate their curricula to facilitate the transition to the regular program.

ESOL students will also be assigned to a team advisor/advisee group and related arts with their buddies. During the remedial reading class in the related arts band, ESOL students will receive support which meets their individual needs in the regular courses, from the reading staff or other available "as assigned" staff.

Students at the advanced level will interact with native English speakers for homeroom, lunch, activity period, related arts, language arts, mathematics, science and social studies.

COMPETENCY

Students who have been exited from the English Acquisition Program will continue in their home schools in the regular academic program. However, these students will have access to the ESOL support tutorial program scheduled at the end of the day. The performance of students who have completed the program will be monitored closely by the ESOL and guidance staff.

HIGH SCHOOL MODEL

GENERAL INFORMATION

The English Acquisition program at the high school level will enhance the current program in three areas: program modifications will better meet the academic needs of all students enrolled in the program, a technology based resource room will be in place to provide an environment for self-study and tutoring, and a mentoring/tutoring program will focus on cross-cultural communication between limited English proficient students and their native English-speaking peers.

The new program design calls for a two-track high school program to meet the academic needs of the *low schooled students* and the *typical learner* students. The courses for low schooled learners will be designated as ESOL 1, ESOL II, ESOL III, and ESOL IV. The low schooled program is designed to give the students a skills-based education which will enable them to have marketable skills and a minimum of an intermediate level of English language proficiency upon graduation.

The typical learner courses will be designed as Trans I, Trans II, and Trans III. The typical learner program is designed to enable the students to participate in mainstream classes 30–40% the first year, upper level mainstream classes at 55% of the time in the second year, 75–80% the third year and exiting the program in the fourth year.

An integral part of this program is the technology-based Resource Room. This room will be set up with computers and a variety of software which will meet the needs of both the low schooled students and the typical learners. Students will be assigned to the Resource Room instead of study halls. There will be diagnostic and prescriptive programs for the students to use to improve their language skills. Software will be available that will enable students to improve skills or explore other academic areas, as well. This Resource Room will also be available for students who have exited the program, but may still be in need of some assistance. At least one professional staff member will be in the room at all times. Students will be encouraged to use this teacher as a resource to assist in doing assignments or for some additional help when needed.

The mentoring/tutoring aspect of the program is the mechanism through which the limited English proficient students will have the opportunity to establish ties with their native English speaking peers. The mentor/tutors will receive special training so they will know how to facilitate communication between themselves and the limited English proficient students. The role of the mentor/tutor will be to assist the new student to become acquainted with the workings and organizations of the school, as well as assisting the student in one or more academic areas. Perhaps more important than the academic aspects of this program are developing mutual understanding and establishing communication links. Philosophically, the concept of home school programming is valued; however, to effectively meet the needs of high school students in both tracks of the program, we recommend that the program continue to be based at the home school. This will assure effective continuity of program implementation, academic focus and staff utilization. At the present time offering two tracks at each high school would fragment learning and limit scheduling flexibility. Additionally, at the high school level, time constraints require that the primary focus be the acquisition of 24.7 credits for graduation. Students must acquire the knowledge necessary to transfer skills to the world of work, the college environment, and the armed services, thus assuring the development of productive citizens.

HIGH SCHOOL PROGRAM OF STUDIES
FOR ENGLISH ACQUISITION STUDENTS

LOW SCHOOLED CATEGORY

ESOL I: Grades 9–10

4 periods:	English Language Development (ESOL staff)
1 period:	Mathematics (ESOL staff)
1 period:	Physical Education/Health/English Acquisition Resource Room
1 period:	English Acquisition Resource Room
1 period:	Elective—Recommending Key-boarding

ESOL II: Grades 10–11

3 periods:	Vocational Technical/Business
1 period:	English Language (ESOL staff)
1 period:	Mathematics—VoTech
1 period:	Science (English through content) (ESOL staff)
1 period:	Social Studies (English through content) (ESOL staff)
1 period:	Physical Education/Health/English Acquisition Resource Room

ESOL III: Grades 10–12

1 period:	English Language Development (ESOL staff)
3 periods:	Vocational/Technical/Business
1 period:	Mathematics—VoTech
1 period:	Science (English through content) (ESOL or regular staff)
1 period:	Social Studies (English through content) (ESOL or regular staff)
1 period:	Physical Education/Health/English Acquisition Resource Room

ESOL IV: Grades 10–12

1 period:	English Language Development (ESOL staff)
3 periods:	Vocational/Technical/Business
1 period:	Science (regular staff)
1 period:	Social Studies (regular staff)
1 period:	Physical Education/English Acquisition Resource Room
1 period:	Mathematics–VoTech

Students may exit into a level appropriate to their academic ability; exiting can occur from Level 3 or Level 4.

TYPICAL LEARNER CATEGORY

TRANS I—Grades 9–11 Mainstream percentage: 30–40%

1 period:	Mathematics—mainstream or with ESOL I
4 periods:	English instruction (integrated reading, listening, oral, and writing) (ESOL staff)
1 period:	Physical Education/Health/English Acquisition Resource Room
1 period:	Elective–Recommending Keyboarding
1 period:	English Acquisition Resource Room

TRANS II—Grades 9–11 Mainstream percentage: 55%

3 periods:	English instruction (integrated reading, listening, oral, and writing) (ESOL staff)
1 period:	Science concepts or social studies concepts; 1 semester each (mainstreamed into regular program)
1 period:	Mathematics
1 period:	Physical Education/Health/English Acquisition Resource Room
1 period:	Foreign language
1 period:	Elective/English Acquisition Resource Room

TRANS III—Grades 9–12 Mainstream percentage: 75–80%—24.7 credits

1 period:	Transitional English: Literature Based (ESOL staff)
1 period:	Content Area Reading (ESOL or regular staff)
1period:	English (B level)
1 period:	Mathematics
1 period:	Science
1 period:	Social Studies
1 period:	Physical Education/Health/English Acquisition Resource Room
1 period:	Electives/English Acquisition Resource Room

APPENDIX D
Sample Interview Questions

MAJOR ORGANIZING QUESTIONS EXPLORED IN THE INTERVIEWS

The major areas helping to establish a broad framework for the interviews were as follows:

1. Daily Interactions With Schools

> Describe the communication that takes place between the school and your family.
> What is a typical conversation between parents and teachers?
> How do you manage interactions with schools?
> What do you do if you are not satisfied with the education your child is receiving?
> What can schools do to enhance the education of bilingual children?
> What can government do to enhance the education of bilingual children?

2. School and Life Experiences

> How do daily school experiences impact family life and routines?
> How do families impact schools?
> What is a typical day in the life of your child?
> What is a typical day in your life?
> What would you like to say about your educational experiences?
> What information needs to be disseminated about the relationship between families and schools?

3. Early Schooling Experiences of Parents and Children

> What would you like to say about your early educational experiences?
> What was it like for you when you attended school?
> What specific experiences do you recall?
> How would you describe your child's early schooling?
> What specific interactions (events, incidents) can you relay that best describe your child's early schooling?

REFERENCES

Ambert, A. (1991). *Bilingual education and English as a second language.* New York: Garland.

Anderson, G. (1989). Critical ethnography in education: Origins, current status, and new directions. *Review of Educational Research, 5*(3), 24–270.

Aronowitz, S., & Giroux, H. (1985). *Education under siege.* South Hadley, Mass.: Bergin & Garvey.

Au, K., & Jordan, C. (1981). Teaching reading to Hawaiian children: Finding a culturally appropriate solution. In H. T. Trueba & G. P. Guthrie (Eds.), *Culture and the bilingual classroom: Studies in classroom ethnography.* Cambridge, Mass.: Newbury House.

Baez, T., Fernandez, R., & Guskin, J. (1980). *Desegregation and Hispanic students: A community perspective.* National Clearinghouse for Bilingual Education. Rosslyn, Va.: InterAmerica Research Associates.

Bain, B. (1974). Bilingualism and cognition: Toward a general theory. In S. Carey (Ed.), *Bilingualism, biculturalism, and education.* Edmonton: University of Alberta.

Bain, B., & Yu, A. (1980). Cognitive consequences of raising children bilingually: One parent, one language. *Canadian Journal of Psychology, 34,* 304–313.

Barrera, R. (1992). Personal communication. Meeting at the National Association for the Education of Young Children, Washington, D.C.

Ben-Zeev, S. (1977). The influence of bilingualism on cognitive strategy and cognitive development. *Child Development, 48,* 1009–1018.

Boyer, D. (November 19, 1992). Bilingual education debaters both want what's best. *Express Times.*

Brendtro, L. K., Brokenleg, M., & Van Bockern, S. (1990). *Reclaiming youth at risk: Our hope for the future.* Bloomington: National Educational Service.

Bronfenbrenner, U., Moen, P., & Garbarino, J. (1984). Child, family, and community. In Ross D. Parke (Ed.), *The family: Review of child development research.* Chicago: University of Chicago Press.

Bronstein, H. (November 16, 1993). School board votes to demolish Calypso, build new school. *Morning Call,* B3.

Bureau of the Census. (1991). The Hispanic population in the U.S.: March, 1991. Washington, D.C.: U.S. Department of Commerce, P-20, no. 455.

Carrasquillo, A. (1991). *Hispanic children and youth in the United States: A resource guide.* New York: Garland.

Cazden, C. (1988). *Classroom discourse: The language of teaching and learning.* Portsmouth, N.H.: Heinemann.

Chapa, J., & Valencia, R. (1993). Latino population growth, demographic characteristics, and education stagnation: An examination of recent trends. *Hispanic Journal of Behavioral Sciences, 15*(2), 165–187.

Collier, C. (November 16, 1992). Bilingual proposal sparks complaint. *Express Times,* A1.

Collier, V. (1992). A synthesis of studies examining long-term language minority student data on academic achievement. *Bilingual Research Journal, 16*(1&2), 187–212.

Collier, V. (1989). How long?: A synthesis of research on academic achievement in a second language. *TESOL Quarterly, 23*(3), 509–531.

Crawford, J. (1992). *Hold your tongue.* New York: Addison-Wesley.

Crawford, J. (1989). *Bilingual education: History, politics, theory and practice.* Trenton, N.J.: Crane.

Cullen, S. (February 12, 1995). It was an experiment that failed. *Patriot News,* Harrisburg, Pa.

Cummins, J. (1994). Keynote speech at the National Association for Bilingual Education, Los Angeles.

Cummins, J. (1993). *Empowering minority students:* A framework for intervention. In L. Weis & M. Fine (Eds.), *Beyond silenced voices* (pp. 101–117). Albany: State University of New York.

Cummins, J. (1989). Empowering minority students. Sacramento: California Association for Bilingual Education.

Cummins, J. (1984). *Bilingualism and special education: Issues in assessment and pedagogy.* Clevedon, Avon, England: Multilingual Matters.

Cummins, J. (1979). Linguistic interdependence and the educational development of bilingual children. *Review of Educational Research, 49*(2), 222–251.

Cummins, J. (1978). Bilingualism and the development of metalinguistic awareness. *Journal of Cross-Cultural Psychology, 9*(2), 131–149.

Cummins, J. (1976). The influence of bilingualism on cognitive growth: A synthesis of research findings and explanatory hypotheses. *Working Papers on Bilingualism, 9,* 1-43.

Cummins, J., & Gulutson, M. (1974). Some effects of bilingualism on cognitive functioning. In S. Carey (Ed.), *Bilingualism, biculturalism and education.* Edmonton: University of Alberta.

Darcy, N. T. (1953). A review of the literature on the effects of bilingualism on the measurement of intelligence. *Journal of Genetic Psychology, 82,* 21–57.

Darder, A. (1991). *Culture and power in the classroom.* Westport, Conn.: Bergin & Garvey.

De Avila, E. (1987). Bilingualism, cognitive function, and language minority group membership. In P. Homel, M. Palij, & D. Aaronson (Eds.), *Childhood bilingualism: Aspects of linguistic, cognitive, and social development* (pp. 149–166). Hillsdale, N.J.: Erlbaum.

Delgado-Gaitan, C. (1990). *Literacy for empowerment: The role of parents in children's education.* New York: Falmer.

Delgado-Gaitan, C., & Trueba, H. (1991). *Crossing cultural borders: Education for immigrant families in America.* New York: Falmer.

Delpit, L. (1993). The silenced dialogue: Power and pedagogy in education of other people's children. In L. Weis & M. Fine (Eds.), *Beyond silenced voices* (pp. 119–139). Albany: State University of New York.

Doluisio, T. (January 27, 1993). Proposal for bilingual education stresses acquiring English early. *Express Times,* A7.

Duncan, S., & De Avila, E. (1979). Bilingualism and cognition. Some recent findings. *NABE Journal, 4,* 15–50.

Emihovich, C. (1994). Editor's preface. *Anthropology and Education Quarterly, 25*(3), 199.

Erickson, F. (1987). Transformation and school success: The politics and culture of educational achievement. *Anthropology and Education Quarterly, 18*(4), 335–356.

Ernst, G., & Statzner, E. (1994). Alternative visions of schooling: An introduction. *Anthropology and Education Quarterly, 25*(3), 200–207.

Ferdman, B. (1991). Literacy and cultural identity. In M. Minami & B. Kennedy (Eds.), *Language issues in literacy and bilingual/multicultural education.* Cambridge: Harvard Educational Review, Reprint series no. 22.

Fernandez, R., Henn-Reinko, K., & Petrovich, J. (1989). Five cities high school dropout study. New York: Aspira

Freire, P. (1970). *Pedagogy of the oppressed.* New York: Seabury.

Freire, P. (1985). *The politics of education: Culture, power, and liberation.* South Hadley, Mass.: Bergin & Garvey.

Freire, P. (1993). *Pedagogy of the city.* New York: Continuum.

Freire, P., & Macedo, D. (1987). *Literacy: Reading the word and the world.* New York: Bergin & Garvey.

Gandara, P. (1994). The impact of the education reform movement on limited English proficient students. In B. McLeod (Ed.), *Language and learning. Educating linguistically diverse students.* Albany: State University of New York.

Giroux, H. (1995). National identity and the politics of multiculturalism. *College Literature, 22*(2), 42–57.

Gomez, M. (1993). Breaking the cycle. *Hispanic, 8,* 12.

Goodenough, F. (1926). Racial diffences in the intelligence of school children. *Journal of Experimental Psychology, 9,* 388–97.

Hakuta, K. (1986). *Mirror of language: The debate of bilingualism.* New York: Basic Books.

Hakuta, K., & Diaz, R. (1985). The relationship between degree of bilingualism and cognitive ability. In K. E. Nelson (Ed.), *Children's language.* Hillsdale, N.J.: Erlbaum.

Hall, M. F. (November 22, 1992). Education shows love, Latino father says. *Morning Call,* B9.

Hall, M. F. (November 19, 1992). Bilingual cut might alter BASD plan. *Morning Call,* A1.

Hall, M. F. (November 14, 1992). Doluisio "surprised" at Latino's response but he cites support for changes in bilingual program. *Morning Call,* B12.

Heath, S. Brice (1983). *Ways with words: Language, life, and work in communities and classrooms.* Cambridge: Cambridge University Press.

Hispanic Policy Development Project. (1986). *The Research Bulletin.* Washington, D.C.

Hodgkinson, H. (1992). *A demographic look at tomorrow.* Washington, D.C.: Institute for Educational Leadership Center for Demographic Policy.

Hodgkinson, H. (1991). Reform versus reality. *Phi Delta Kappan, 73*(1), 8–16.

Hodgkinson, H. (1985). *All one system: Demographics of education, kindergarten through graduate school.* Washington, D.C.: Institute for Educational Leadership Center for Demographic Policy.

Ianco-Worral, A. (1972). Bilingualism and cognitive development. *Child Development,* 43, 1390–1400.

Jensen, V. (1962). Effects of childhood bilingualism, I. *Elementary English, 39,* 132–143.

Kennedy, John F. (1962). Speech at Yale University, New Haven, Conn.

Kopacki, J. (January 5, 1993). Bilingual education meeting set. *Express Times,* B1.

Krashen, S. (1988). *On course.* Sacramento: California Association for Bilingual Education.

Kupper, T. (November 13, 1992). Hispanics object to BASD language plan. *Morning Call,* B1.

Lambert, W. (1975). Culture and language as factors in learning and education. In A. Wolfgang (Ed.), *Education of immigrant students.* Toronto: Ontario Institute for Studies in Education.

Lambert, W. E., & Tucker, G. R. (1972). *Bilingual education of children: The St. Lambert Experiment.* Rowley, Mass.: Newbury House.

Lather, P. (1986). Research as praxis. *Harvard Educational Review, 56*(3), 257–277.

Leopold, W. (1939). *Speech development of a bilingual child: A linguist's record, vol. 1, Vocabulary growth in the first two years.* Evanston, Ill.: Northwestern University.

Lewis, E. G. (1980). *Bilingualism and bilingual education: A comparative study.* Albuquerque: University of New Mexico Press.

Liedtke, W., & Nelson, L. (1968). Concept formation in bilingualism. *Alberta Journal of Educational Research, 14,* 225–232.

Lopez, A. (1995). Personal communication. Meetings of California Tomorrow, San Francisco.

Lucas, T., Henze, R., & Donato, R. (1990). Promoting the success of Latino language-minority students: An exploratory study of six high schools. In M. Minami & B. Kennedy (Eds.),

Language issues in literacy and bilingual/multicultural education. Cambridge: Harvard Educational Review, Reprint series no. 22.

Macedo, D. (1994). *Literacies of power: What Americans are not allowed to know.* Boulder: Westview.

Macias, J. (1987). The hidden curriculum of Papago teachers. In G. & L. Spindler (Eds.), *Interpretive ethnography of education* (pp. 363–384). Hillsdale, N.J.: Erlbaum.

Martin, J. P. (January 29, 1993). Liberty crowd urges keeping bilingual program. *Morning Call,* B1, B5.

Martin, J. P. (January 28, 1993). Public to have say on bilingual issue. *Morning Call,* B1, B7.

Martin, J. P. (December 16, 1992). Public input must wait in BASD facilities, bilingual matters to be heard in late January. *Morning Call,* B3.

Martin, J. P. (December 15, 1992). School board limits time members may talk on issues. *Morning Call,* B3.

Martin, J. P. (November 30, 1992). School ponders bilingual mainstreaming. *Morning Call,* B1.

Martin, J. P. (November 30, 1992). Bilingual education hot in Steel Town, does it help Spanish speakers learn, or just keep them separated, debate asks. *Morning Call,* B4.

Martin, J. P. (November 30, 1992). Two-way bilingual programs grow in popularity. *Morning Call,* B5.

Martin, J. P. (November 10, 1992). Bilingual program headed for change. *Morning Call* .A1.

Martin, J. P. & Hall, M. Floyd. (November 30, 1992). Bilingual education hot in Steeltown! *Morning Call,* B4.

McLaren, P. (1994). *Life in schools: An introduction to critical pedagogy in the foundations of education.* New York: Longman.

McLaughlin, B. (1984). *Second-language acquisition in childhood.* Hillsdale, N.J.: Erlbaum.

Mehan, H. (1994). The role of discourse in learning, schooling, and reform. In B. McLeod (Ed.), *Language and learning: Educating linguistically diverse students.* Albany: State University of New York.

Mehan, H., Hubbard, L., & Villanueva, I. (1994). Forming academic identities: Accommodation without assimilation among involuntary minorities. *Anthropology and Education Quarterly, 25*(2), 91–117.

Messinger, C. (1995). Lenni Lenape Historical Society, Allentown, Pa. Personal communication.

Miranda, L. (1991). *Latino child poverty in the United States.* Washington, D.C.: Children's Defense Fund.

Miranda, L., & Quiroz, J. T. (1990). *The decade of the Hispanic: An economic retrospective.* Washington, D.C.: National Council of La Raza.

Moll, L., & Diaz, S. (1987). Change as a goal of educational research. *Anthropology and Education Quarterly, 18,* 300–311.

Morales, J. (January 25, 1992). Prolonged bilingual programs put Latinos at a disadvantage. *Morning Call,* A9.

Morning Call. (February 5, 1993). It's the district's responsibility to do whatever it can to help students succeed, A12.

Morning Call. (November 22, 1992). Untangle bilingual, other issues, A26.

Mulligan, B. (June 14, 1993). Board to decide on what to teach English-lacking. *Express Times,* B1, B5.

Mulligan, B. (February 19, 1993). Bilingual education addressed. *Express Times,* B1.

Mulligan, B. (February 3, 1993). Picking up the pieces after bilingual battle. *Express Times,* B1.

Mulligan, B. (February 1993). School to immerse in English. *Express Times,* A1, A2.

Mulligan, B. (January 30, 1993). Bilingual education up in air. *Express Times,* A1, A2.

Mulligan, B. (January 29, 1993). Cheers, boos, prayer at bilingual meeting. *Express Times,* A1, A2.

Mulligan, B. (January 28, 1993). Students defend Spanish program. *Express Times,* A1, A2.

Mulligan, B. (January 12, 1993). Doluisio pushes ideas on bilingual education. *Express Times,* B1, B2.

Ogbu, J. (1978). *Minority education and caste.* New York: Academic.

Ortiz, A., & Yates, J. (1983). Incidence of exceptionality among Hispanics: Implications for manpower planning. *NABE Journal, 7,* 41–54.

Otheguy, R. (1991). Thinking about bilingual education: A critical appraisal. In M. Minami & B. Kennedy (Eds.), *Language issues in literacy and bilingual/multicultural education.* Cambridge: Harvard Educational Review, Reprint series no. 22.

Partnership for Community Health in the Lehigh Valley. (1993). Major Health Problems in the Lehigh Valley. Preliminary report. Lehigh Valley, Pa.

Paul, B., & Jarvis, C. (1992). *The effects of native language use in New York City prekindergarten classes.* Paper presented at the American Educational Research Association, San Francisco.

Peal, E., & Lambert, W. (1962). The relation of bilingualism to intelligence. *Psychological Monographs: General and Applied, 76*(27, whole no. 546), 1–23.

Peck, B. (1993). The language explosion: Europe starts it early. *Phi Delta Kappan, 9,* 91–92.

Phillips, S. (1983). *The invisible culture: Communication in classroom and community on the Warm Springs Reservation.* New York: Longman.

Politi, N. (November 16, 1992). Latino leaders file complaint against BASD. *Morning Call,* A1.

President's Commission on Foreign Languages and International Studies (1980). *Strength through wisdom: A critique of U.S. Capability.* Washington, D.C.: U.S. Government Printing Office.

Ramirez, M., & Casteneda, A. (1974). *Cultural democracy: Bicognitive development and education.* New York: Academic.

Ronjat, J. (1913). *Le development du language observe chez un enfant bilingue.* Paris: Champion.

Ruiz, N., Figueroa, R., Rueda, R, & Beaumont, C. (1992). History and status of bilingual special education for Hispanic handicapped students. In R. Padilla & A. Benavides (Eds.), *Critical perspectives on bilingual education research.* Tempe: Bilingual Review/Press.

Saer, D. J. (1923). The effects of bilingualism on intelligence. *British Journal of Psychology, 14,* 25–38.

Sanchez-Cintron, I (Chair). (1993). Updated report to Governor's Advisory Commission on Latino Affairs. Harrisburg, Pa: GACLA.

Schnur, B. (December 9, 1992). Bilingual dispute continues in city. *Express Times,* B1–B2.

Schnur, B. (November 21, 1992). Debate continues on how to teach Latino students. *Express Times,* B1–B2.

Schnur, B. (November 21, 1992). Bilingual program has many languages. *Express Times,* B1–B2.

Schnur, B. (November 19, 1992). School space needs hinge on bilingual program. *Express Times,* B1.

Schnur, B. (November 17, 1992). Bilingual program to be studied. *Express Times,* A1, A2.

Schnur, B. (November 14, 1992). Bilingual program debated. *Express Times,* B1, B2.

Schnur, B. (November 13, 1992). Civil rights complaint threatened. *Express Times,* A1, A2.

Schnur, B. (November 10, 1992). Doluisio criticizes bilingual program. *Express Times,* A1, A2.

Schwarz, R. G. (1992). *Bethlehem on the Lehigh.* Bethlehem, Pa: Bethlehem Area Foundation.

Schweinhart, L. (1994). Lasting benefits of preschool programs. Eric Digest (EDO-PS-94-2).

Skutnabb-Kangas, T. (1989). *Bilingualism or not: The education of minorities.* Clevedon, England: Multilingual Matters, Ltd.

Sleeter, C. E., & Grant, C. A. (1992). *Making choices for multicultural education.* 2nd ed. Columbus, Ohio: Merrill.

Snyder, S. (November 22, 1992). Latinos fight for equality in area schools: Officials grapple with problems, disagree on workable solutions. *Morning Call,* B1.

Snyder, S. (November 18, 1992). Bilingual education is questioned: Educators debate value of classes in Spanish. *Morning Call,* B1.

Soto, L. D. (1994). The early education of linguistically and culturally diverse children. Boston: National Coalition of Advocates for Students.

Soto, L. D. (1993). Native language for school success. *Bilingual Research Journal, 17*(1&2), 83–97.

Soto, L. D. (1992a). Success stories. In C. Grant (Ed.), *Research and multicultural education.* London: Falmer.

Soto, L. D. (1992b). Alternate paradigms in bilingual education research. In R. Padilla & A. Benavides (Eds.), *Critical perspectives on bilingual education research.* Tempe, Ariz.: Bilingual Press/Editorial Bilingüe.

Soto, L. D. (November 17, 1992). English-only classrooms don't meet needs of a diverse society. *Morning Call*, B1.

Spindler, G., & Spindler, L. (Eds.). (1987). *Interpretive Ethnography of Education*. Hillsdale, N.J.: Erlbaum.

Spiro, P. (1994). Cause and effect. In M. Algarin & B. Holman (Eds.), *Aloud: Voices from the Nuyorican Poets' Café*. New York: Henry Holt.

Spradley, J. P. (1980). *Participant observation*. New York: Holt, Rinehart & Winston.

Spradley, J. P. (1979). *The ethnographic interview*. New York: Holt, Rinehart & Winston.

Strauss, A., & Corbin, J. (1990). *Basics of qualitative research: Grounded theory procedures and techniques*. Newbury Park: Sage.

Swain, M. (1987). Bilingual education: Research and its implications. In M. Long & J. Richards (Eds.), *Methodology in TESOL*. Cambridge, Mass.: Newbury House.

Torrance, E., Wu, J., & Alliotti, N. (1970). Creating functioning of monolingual and bilingual children in Singapore. *Journal of Educational Psychology, 61,* 72–75.

Trueba, H. T., Jacobs, L., & Kirton, E. (1990). *Cultural conflict and adaptation: The case of Hmong children in American society*. New York: Falmer.

Trueba, H. T. (Ed.). (1987). *Success and failure: Learning and the linguistic minority student*. Cambridge, Mass.: Newbury House.

Valdivieso, R., & Davis, C. (1989). U.S. Hispanics: Challenging issues for the 1990's. Washington, D.C.: Hispanic Policy Development Project.

W-B Olsen, R. E. (1993). *Enrollment statistics of limited English proficient students in the United States*. Alexandria, Va.: TESOL Field Services.

Waggoner, D. (1993). The growth of multilingualism and the need for bilingual education: What do we know so far? *Bilingual Research Journal, 17*(1, 2), 1–12.

Wang, L. (1980). Lau v. Nichols: History of a struggle for equal and quality education. In *Asian-Americans: Social and psychological perspectives*. Vol. 2. Palo Alto, Ca.: Behavior Books.

Weinreich, U. (1953). *Languages in contact: Findings and problems*. New York: Linguistic Circle of New York. Reprinted by Mouton, The Hague, 1974.

Williams, T. (January 24, 1993). Ethnic barriers not insurmountable. *Express Times*, B1.

Williams, T. (January 23, 1993). Latino leader wants 800 at hearing. *Express Times*, B1, B4.

Willig, A. (1985). A meta-analysis of selected studies on the effectiveness of bilingual education. *Review of Educational Research, 55*(3), 269–317.

Witmer, L. (February 12, 1995). In S. Cullen, It was an experiment that failed. *Patriot News*, Harrisburg, Pa., B1–3.

Wong Fillmore, L. (in press). Learning a language from learners. In C. Kramsch & S. McConnell-Ginet (Eds.), *Cross-disciplinary perspectives on language studies*. Lexington, Mass.: D. C. Heath.

Wong Fillmore, L. (1992). Language and cultural issues in early education. In L. L. Kagan

(Ed.), *The care and education of America's young children.* The 90th Yearbook of the National Society for the Study of Education.

Wong Fillmore, L. (1991). When learning a second language means losing the first. *Early Childhood Research Quarterly, 6,* 323–346.

Worrick, D. (November 20, 1992). Superintendent right on bilingual education. *Morning Call,* A18.

Yzaguirre, R. (1992). *State of Hispanic America 1991: An overview.* Washington, D.C.: National Council of La Raza.

Zelasko, N. (Ed.). (1993). Census reports sharp increase in number of non-English language speaking Americans. National Association for Bilingual Education. *NABE NEWS, 16*(3), 1–25.

AUTHOR INDEX

SUBJECT INDEX